READ UP

1

on Content Areas

NE_Build & Grow

Unit Components

Building Background Knowledge prepares students for the reading passage by providing additional topic information and visual aids.

On Your Own applies points from the text to students' lives.

The Big Question prompts students to think about the main idea of the passage.

Visual Aids provide more information about the main text and help students understand the passage with additional illustrations and photographs.

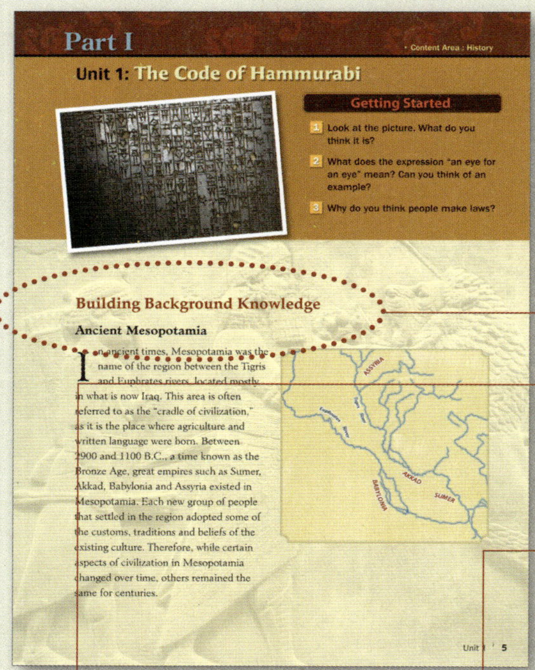

Part I · Content Area : History

Unit 1: The Code of Hammurabi

Getting Started

1. Look at the picture. What do you think it is?
2. What does the expression "an eye for an eye" mean? Can you think of an example?
3. Why do you think people make laws?

Building Background Knowledge

Ancient Mesopotamia

In ancient times, Mesopotamia was the name of the region between the Tigris and Euphrates rivers, located mostly in what is now Iraq. This area is often referred to as the "cradle of civilization," as it is the place where agriculture and written language were born. Between 2900 and 1100 B.C., a time known as the Bronze Age, great empires such as Sumer, Akkad, Babylonia and Assyria existed in Mesopotamia. Each new group of people that settled in the region adopted some of the customs, traditions and beliefs of the existing culture. Therefore, while certain aspects of civilization in Mesopotamia changed over time, others remained the same for centuries.

Unit 1 5

UNIT 1

The Code of Hammurabi

The Big Question

Why was Hammurabi's code of laws so important?

The ancient region of Mesopotamia was ruled by many **empires**. Before 2000 B.C., the Akkadian Empire was the most powerful. Soon after this, however, the Akkadians were conquered by a people called the Amorites. The Amorite capital was a city named Babylon, located in modern-day Iraq. Therefore, the empire they built became known as the Babylonian Empire.

Life in the Babylonian Empire was very orderly. The kings of Babylon built **irrigation canals**, defensive walls, massive public buildings, and street **grids**. They also started one of the earliest systems of **taxation** to collect money from Babylonian citizens. The most famous king of Babylon was Hammurabi. Although he was a great warrior, he is better remembered for something else: the Code of Hammurabi.

▲ Babylon is thought to have been the world's largest city during the time periods of 1770 to 1670 B.C. and 612 to 320 B.C. It may have been the first city with a population exceeding 200,000.

Hammurabi's code was a collection of laws that were written down and put on display for everyone to see. It not only described what was against the law but also what **punishments** would be given to lawbreakers. For example, the code stated that stealing property from temples was illegal.

empire many lands that are ruled by one leader
irrigation canal a path made for water to be used for crops
grid a pattern of lines that are crossed in a planned way
taxation a requirement that people pay money to their government

8

It also said that anyone caught doing this would be put to death. The range of the code was quite broad, covering issues from money lending to military service.

Some of the 281 laws in the code came from Amorite tradition. Others were borrowed from earlier empires, such as the Akkadians. Still others were brand new. The principle of "an eye for an eye" was an example of a new method of **justice**. If people caused others harm, they would be punished by having the same type of harm inflicted on them. Many copies of Hammurabi's code were written on large **slabs** of stone or wood and placed in public areas. This was the first time a **government**'s laws had been explained and distributed like this.

Eventually, the Babylonian Empire fell, just as its predecessors had. It was conquered by the Kassites, a people from present-day Iran. But the Kassites didn't destroy Babylon. In fact, they adopted many elements of Babylonian culture, including the Code of Hammurabi. In this way, the code was passed from empire to empire, guiding the development of different legal systems. Its influence can even be seen in the laws we follow today.

▲ The Code of Hammurabi carved on a slab

On Your Own

What kinds of rules do your parents make you follow at home?

punishment unpleasant consequences for actions that break laws or rules
justice maintaining fairness among people
slab a thick piece of material like stone or wood
government an organization that has political rule over a certain area or population

Unit 1 9

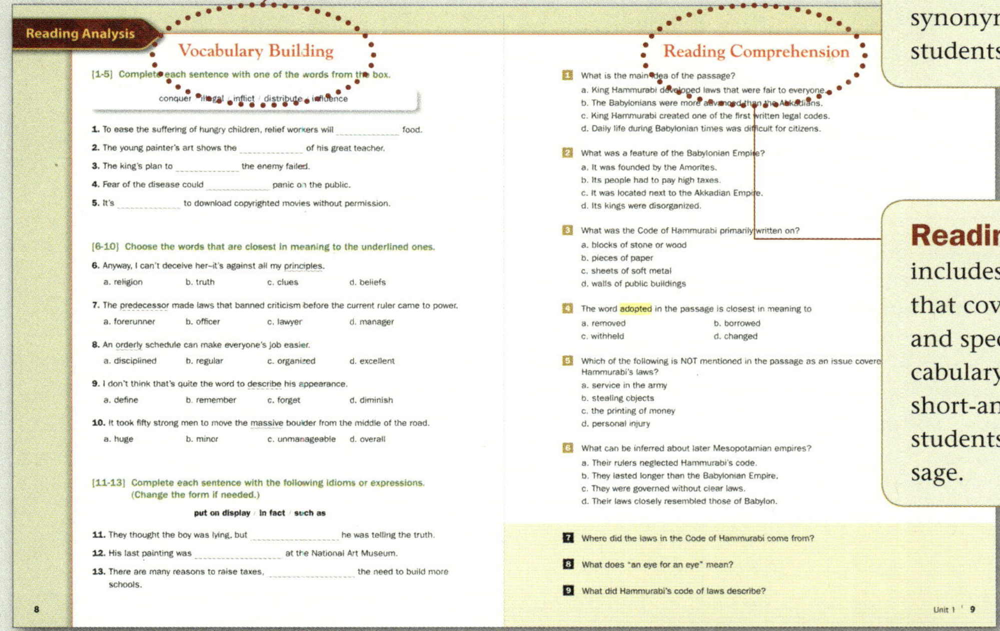

Reading Analysis

Vocabulary Building

[1-5] Complete each sentence with one of the words from the box.

conquer / illegal / inflict / distribute / influence

1. To ease the suffering of hungry children, relief workers will __________ food.
2. The young painter's art shows the __________ of his great teacher.
3. The king's plan to __________ the enemy failed.
4. Fear of the disease could __________ panic on the public.
5. It's __________ to download copyrighted movies without permission.

[6-10] Choose the words that are closest in meaning to the underlined ones.

6. Anyway, I can't deceive her–it's against all my principles.
   a. religion b. truth c. clues d. beliefs
7. The predecessor made laws that banned criticism before the current ruler came to power.
   a. forerunner b. officer c. lawyer d. manager
8. An orderly schedule can make everyone's job easier.
   a. disciplined b. regular c. organized d. excellent
9. I don't think that's quite the word to describe his appearance.
   a. define b. remember c. forget d. diminish
10. It took fifty strong men to move the massive boulder from the middle of the road.
   a. huge b. minor c. unmanageable d. overall

[11-13] Complete each sentence with the following idioms or expressions. (Change the form if needed.)

put on display / in fact / such as

11. They thought the boy was lying, but __________ he was telling the truth.
12. His last painting was __________ at the National Art Museum.
13. There are many reasons to raise taxes, __________ the need to build more schools.

8

Reading Comprehension

1 What is the main idea of the passage?
a. King Hammurabi developed laws that were fair to everyone.
b. The Babylonians were more advanced than the Akkadians.
c. King Hammurabi created one of the first written legal codes.
d. Daily life during Babylonian times was difficult for citizens.

2 What was a feature of the Babylonian Empire?
a. It was founded by the Amorites.
b. Its people had to pay high taxes.
c. It was located next to the Akkadian Empire.
d. Its kings were disorganized.

3 What was the Code of Hammurabi primarily written on?
a. blocks of stone or wood
b. pieces of paper
c. sheets of soft metal
d. walls of public buildings

4 The word adopted in the passage is closest in meaning to
a. removed b. borrowed
c. withheld d. changed

5 Which of the following is NOT mentioned in the passage as an issue covered by Hammurabi's laws?
a. service in the army
b. stealing objects
c. the printing of money
d. personal injury

6 What can be inferred about later Mesopotamian empires?
a. Their rulers neglected Hammurabi's code.
b. They lasted longer than the Babylonian Empire.
c. They were governed without clear laws.
d. Their laws closely resembled those of Babylon.

7 Where did the laws in the Code of Hammurabi come from?

8 What does "an eye for an eye" mean?

9 What did Hammurabi's code of laws describe?

Unit 1 9

Vocabulary Building

presents new words in context, synonyms, and idioms to improve students' vocabulary.

Reading Comprehension

includes multiple-choice questions that cover the main idea, general and specific information, and vocabulary. Negative, inference, and short-answer questions further test students' understanding of the passage.

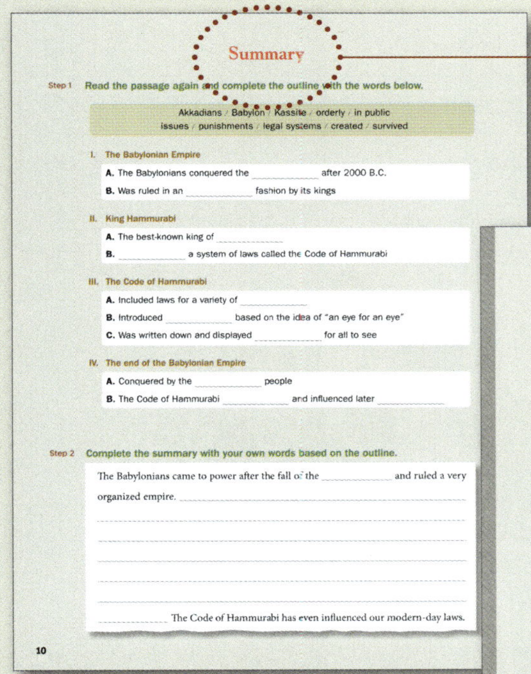

Summary

Step 1 Read the passage again and complete the outline with the words below.

Akkadians / Babylon / Kassite / orderly / in public
issues / punishments / legal systems / created / survived

I. The Babylonian Empire
A. The Babylonians conquered the __________ after 2000 B.C.
B. Was ruled in an __________ fashion by its kings

II. King Hammurabi
A. The best-known king of __________
B. __________ a system of laws called the Code of Hammurabi

III. The Code of Hammurabi
A. Included laws for a variety of __________
B. Introduced __________ based on the idea of "an eye for an eye"
C. Was written down and displayed __________ for all to see

IV. The end of the Babylonian Empire
A. Conquered by the __________ people
B. The Code of Hammurabi __________ and influenced later __________

Step 2 Complete the summary with your own words based on the outline.

The Babylonians came to power after the fall of the __________ and ruled a very organized empire. __________

__________ The Code of Hammurabi has even influenced our modern-day laws.

10

Summary

Step 1 Completing an outline

Step 2 Writing a summary based on the information from Step 1

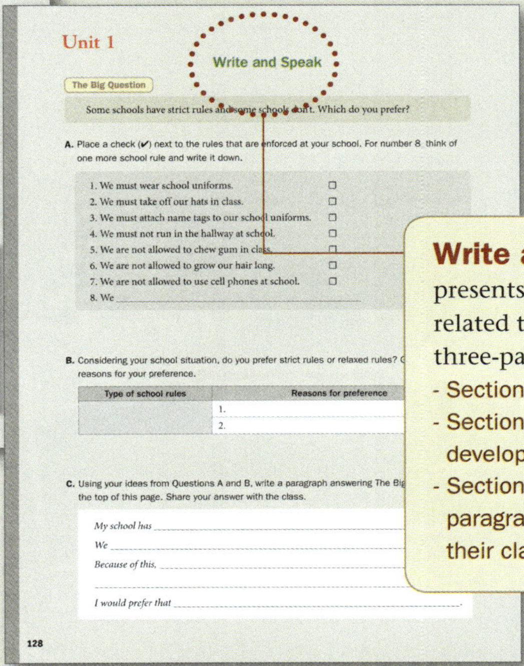

Unit 1

Write and Speak

The Big Question

Some schools have strict rules and some schools don't. Which do you prefer?

A. Place a check (✔) next to the rules that are enforced at your school. For number 8, think of one more school rule and write it down.

1. We must wear school uniforms. ☐
2. We must take off our hats in class. ☐
3. We must attach name tags to our school uniforms. ☐
4. We must not run in the hallway at school. ☐
5. We are not allowed to chew gum in class. ☐
6. We are not allowed to grow our hair long. ☐
7. We are not allowed to use cell phones at school. ☐
8. We __________

B. Considering your school situation, do you prefer strict rules or relaxed rules? G... reasons for your preference.

Type of school rules	Reasons for preference
	1.
	2.

C. Using your ideas from Questions A and B, write a paragraph answering The Big ... the top of this page. Share your answer with the class.

My school has __________
We __________
Because of this, __________
____
I would prefer that __________.

128

Write and Speak

presents students with a question related to the passage followed by a three-part writing exercise.

- Section A is a warm-up activity
- Section B helps students form and develop their ideas
- Section C asks students to write a paragraph that they will share with their class

Contents

Part I

Part II

Part III

Part IV

Part I

Unit 1: The Code of Hammurabi

Getting Started

1. Look at the picture. What do you think it is?
2. What does the expression "an eye for an eye" mean? Can you think of an example?
3. Why do you think people make laws?

Building Background Knowledge

Ancient Mesopotamia

In ancient times, Mesopotamia was the name of the region between the Tigris and Euphrates rivers, located mostly in what is now Iraq. This area is often referred to as the "cradle of civilization," as it is the place where agriculture and written language were born. Between 2900 and 1100 B.C., a time known as the Bronze Age, great empires such as Sumer, Akkad, Babylonia, and Assyria existed in Mesopotamia. Each new group of people that settled in the region adopted some of the customs, traditions and beliefs of the existing culture. Therefore, while certain aspects of civilization in Mesopotamia changed over time, others remained the same for centuries.

▲ Map of ancient Mesopotamia

UNIT 1

The Code of Hammurabi

The Big Question

Why was Hammurabi's code of laws so important?

► Notes

The ancient region of Mesopotamia was ruled by many **empires**. Before 2000 B.C., the Akkadian Empire was the most powerful. Soon after this, however, the Akkadians were conquered by a people called the Amorites. The Amorite capital was a city named Babylon, located in modern-day Iraq. Therefore, the empire they built became known as the Babylonian Empire.

Life in the Babylonian Empire was very orderly. The kings of Babylon built **irrigation canals**, defensive walls, massive public buildings, and street **grids**. They also started one of the earliest systems of **taxation** to collect money from Babylonian citizens. The most famous king of Babylon was Hammurabi. Although he was a great warrior, he is better remembered for something else: the Code of Hammurabi.

▲ Babylon is thought to have been the world's largest city during the time periods of 1770 to 1670 B.C. and 612 to 320 B.C. It may have been the first city with a population exceeding 200,000.

Hammurabi's code was a collection of laws that were written down and put on display for everyone to see. It not only described what was against the law but also what **punishments** would be given to lawbreakers. For example, the code stated that stealing property from temples was illegal.

empire many lands that are ruled by one leader
irrigation canal a path made for water to be used for crops
grid a pattern of lines that are crossed in a planned way
taxation a requirement that people pay money to their government

It also said that anyone caught doing this would be put to death. The range of the code was quite broad, covering issues from money lending to military service.

Some of the 281 laws in the code came from Amorite tradition. Others were borrowed from earlier empires, such as the Akkadians. Still others were brand new. The principle of "an eye for an eye" was an example of a new method of **justice**. If people caused others harm, they would be punished by having the same type of harm inflicted on them. Many copies of Hammurabi's code were written on large **slabs** of stone or wood and placed in public areas. This was the first time a **government**'s laws had been explained and distributed like this.

Eventually, the Babylonian Empire fell, just as its predecessors had. It was conquered by the Kassites, a people from present-day Iran. But the Kassites didn't destroy Babylon. In fact, they adopted many elements of Babylonian culture, including the Code of Hammurabi. In this way, the code was passed from empire to empire, guiding the development of different legal systems. Its influence can even be seen in the laws we follow today.

► Notes

▲The Code of Hammurabi carved on a slab

On Your Own

What kinds of rules do your parents make you follow at home?

punishment unpleasant consequences for actions that break laws or rules

justice maintaining fairness among people

slab a thick piece of material like stone or wood

government an organization that has political rule over a certain area or population

Vocabulary Building

[1-5] Complete each sentence with one of the words from the box.

conquer / illegal / inflict / distribute / influence

1. Relief workers will ______________ food to hungry children.

2. The young painter's art shows the ______________ of his great teacher.

3. The king's plan to ______________ the enemy failed.

4. Bullies like to ______________ harm on others.

5. It's ______________ to download copyrighted movies without permission.

[6-10] Choose the words that are closest in meaning to the underlined ones.

6. I won't deceive her because it's against all my <u>principles</u>.

a. religion b. truth c. clues d. beliefs

7. The <u>predecessor</u> made laws that banned criticism before the current ruler came to power.

a. forerunner b. officer c. lawyer d. manager

8. An <u>orderly</u> schedule can make everyone's job easier.

a. disciplined b. regular c. organized d. excellent

9. I don't think that's quite the word to <u>describe</u> his appearance.

a. define b. remember c. forget d. diminish

10. It took fifty strong men to move the <u>massive</u> rock from the middle of the road.

a. huge b. minor c. unmanageable d. overall

[11-13] Complete each sentence with the following idioms.

put on display / in fact / such as

11. They thought the boy was lying, but ________________ he was telling the truth.

12. His last painting was ________________ at the National Art Museum.

13. There are many reasons to raise taxes, ________________ the need to build more schools.

Reading Comprehension

1 What is the main idea of the passage?

a. King Hammurabi developed laws that were fair to everyone.
b. The Babylonians were more advanced than the Akkadians.
c. King Hammurabi created one of the first written legal codes.
d. Daily life during Babylonian times was difficult for citizens.

2 According to the passage, what was a feature of the Babylonian Empire?

a. It was founded by the Amorites.
b. Its people had to pay high taxes.
c. It was located next to the Akkadian Empire.
d. Its kings were disorganized.

3 What was the Code of Hammurabi primarily written on?

a. blocks of stone or wood
b. pieces of paper
c. sheets of soft metal
d. walls of public buildings

4 The word adopted in the passage is closest in meaning to

a. removed   b. borrowed
c. withheld   d. changed

5 Which of the following is NOT mentioned in the passage as an issue covered by Hammurabi's laws?

a. service in the army
b. stealing objects
c. the printing of money
d. personal injury

6 What can be inferred about later Mesopotamian empires?

a. Their rulers neglected Hammurabi's code.
b. They lasted longer than the Babylonian Empire.
c. They were governed without clear laws.
d. Their laws closely resembled those of Babylon.

7 Where did the laws in the Code of Hammurabi come from?

8 What does "an eye for an eye" mean?

9 What did Hammurabi's code of laws describe?

Summary

Step 1 **Read the passage again and complete the outline with the words below.**

Akkadians / Babylon / Kassite / orderly / in public issues / punishments / legal systems / created / survived

I. The Babylonian Empire

A. The Amorites conquered the ____________ around 2000 B.C.

B. Babylon was ruled in a(n) ____________ fashion by its kings

II. King Hammurabi

A. The best-known king of ____________

B. ____________ a system of laws called the Code of Hammurabi

III. The Code of Hammurabi

A. Included laws for a variety of ____________

B. Introduced ____________ based on the idea of "an eye for an eye"

C. Was written down and displayed ____________ for all to see

IV. The end of the Babylonian Empire

A. Conquered by the ____________ people

B. The Code of Hammurabi ____________ and influenced later ____________

Step 2 **Complete the summary with your own words based on the outline.**

The Amorites conquered the ____________ around 2000 B.C. and ruled Babylon in a(n) ____________ fashion. ____

____

____

____

____

____

____ The Code of Hammurabi ____________ and influenced later ____________.

Unit 2: The Three Climate Zones of West and Central Africa

Getting Started

1. Where do you think this picture was taken? Can you describe the area?
2. When you think about Africa, what comes to mind first?
3. Have you ever visited a region with a climate that was very different from where you live? What was it like?

Building Background Knowledge

The Climates of Africa

Africa is the earth's second largest continent, accounting for approximately one fifth of the planet's land and covering a number of different climate zones. Generally, the continent is quite warm throughout most of the year, but there are more moderate temperatures in some mountainous and coastal areas. The overall range of climates is extreme, ranging from tropical conditions to subarctic ones on the highest mountain peaks. Most of Africa's northern half consists of either desert or arid regions, while plains and jungles cover the central and southern parts. Between these two distinct climate zones is a third region where they meet, known as the Sahel. This region is a belt that stretches 1,000 kilometers across the continent, from the Atlantic Ocean to the Red Sea.

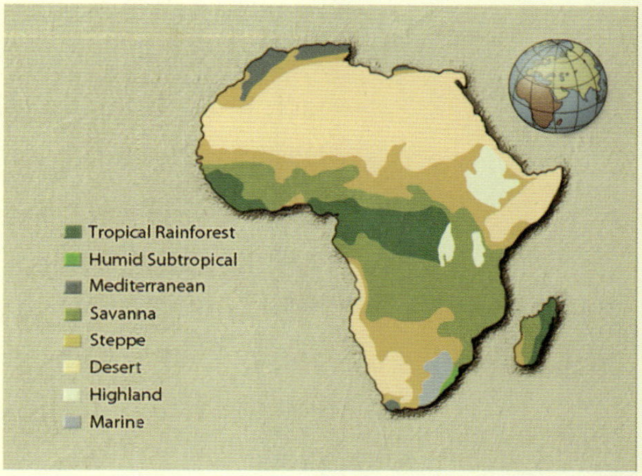

▲ Regional climates of the African continent

UNIT 2

The Three Climate Zones of West and Central Africa

The Big Question

What is the main difference between the Sahel, the savanna, and the rainforest?

▸ Notes

If you were to travel across West and Central Africa, you would see the landscape and **climate** change a lot during your journey. You might visit rocky **plains**, green fields, and forests full of tall trees. This is because there are three very different **ecological** zones in this part of the world: the Sahel, the savanna, and the rainforest. The amount of rainfall is the main difference between each zone.

What would you see if you traveled to the Sahel? The landscape is mostly flat and sandy with very few bodies of water, like a desert. In fact, it is a **transitional** zone between the Sahara Desert to the north and the grasslands to the south. It shares characteristics with both deserts and grasslands. Like a desert, it receives very little rainfall. However, some parts of the Sahel are covered in short grasses, and there is just enough water for some trees and tough plants to grow.

▲ Rainforest

South of the Sahel lies the savanna, a huge grassy **plateau** dotted with trees. One of the most important features of this ecological zone is its rainy season. Although this region is very dry for part of the year, summer rains transform the savanna into an **oasis**. Because of this, many kinds of **vegetation** that cannot survive in the dry Sahel grow in the savanna.

West Africa's rainforest region can be found even farther south. There,

climate the pattern of weather in an area of the world
plain a large area of land that is mostly flat and dry
ecological related to the interaction between plants and animals and their environment
transitional related to conditions that are changing

the climate is wet and **tropical**, making it an ideal environment for all kinds of vegetation. More than 500 centimeters of rain fall every year, so the landscape is very green and crowded with tall trees. The trees are so close together that their leaves act like a roof over the forest below.

These climates greatly affect people's lives. In this part of the world, many must grow their own food in order to survive. But farmers in all three zones face many difficulties. In the Sahel, people must travel great distances to find enough water for survival. Because of climate change and poor agricultural practices like overgrazing, the Sahel gets drier every year, and life becomes harder. In the savanna, people plan their farming activities around the rainy season. They must always be thinking ahead. Even the rainforest is a hard place to live. The trees are so close together that people have little room for crops, so it can be hard to grow enough food.

▲ Overgrazing is an environmentally harmful agricultural practice that occurs when too many domesticated animals are kept in an area or when their grazing is not properly controlled. It damages plants and weakens the soil.

▸ Notes

On Your Own

What is the climate like where you live?

plateau an area of land that is mostly flat and at a higher elevation than the area surrounding it
oasis a place in a desert with water and trees
vegetation the plant life in a certain area
tropical of or occurring in a moist and generally warm climate

Vocabulary Building

[1-5] Complete each sentence with one of the words from the box.

flat / survive / ideal / distances / landscape

1. It is too costly to travel long ______________ by car.

2. If we want eagles to ______________, we must respect their natural habitat.

3. The mountainous ______________ is rocky and varied.

4. The day after the destructive storm, the sea was ______________ and calm.

5. The house is in a(n) ______________ location near my job and my parents.

[6-10] Choose the words that are closest in meaning to the underlined ones.

6. People who care about the environment are against the use of plastic bags.

a. ecosystem b. issue c. revival d. leadership

7. I hope he will not let his feelings about me affect his decision.

a. influence b. blame c. convince d. consider

8. A characteristic of that breed of dog is friendliness.

a. advantage b. pastime c. trait d. reputation

9. I am waiting to receive news about whether I have been accepted.

a. advertise b. divide c. gather d. get

10. Local farmers lost their crops due to unexpected freezing cold temperatures.

a. food b. produce c. soil d. sales

[11-13] Complete each sentence with the following idioms.

think ahead / be crowded with / have little room for

11. The market ____________________ buyers and sellers yesterday.

12. Have you ____________________ about what you will do for vacation in the spring?

13. We found that we ____________________ the new furniture in our apartment.

Reading Comprehension

1 What is the main idea of the passage?

a. West and Central Africa receive very little rainfall.
b. The Sahel is the most difficult zone of West and Central Africa to live in.
c. Farmers in Africa face a number of environmental pressures.
d. There are three distinct climates in West and Central Africa.

2 Which of the following landscapes best represents the Sahel?

a. a rocky plateau covered with tall trees
b. grassland dotted with small lakes and rivers
c. sandy or grassy plains with minimal vegetation
d. a desert that has been largely converted into farmland

3 What makes the rainforest zone a difficult place for growing crops?

a. There is not enough space for agricultural activities.
b. Heavy rainfall makes the soil too wet for farming.
c. There are not enough natural bodies of water to support crops.
d. Wild animals consume the crops before they can be harvested.

4 The word transform in the passage is closest in meaning to

a. hold b. change
c. repeat d. limit

5 Which of the following is NOT mentioned in the passage as a problem faced by West and Central African farmers?

a. an overabundance of trees
b. an unstable population
c. irregular rainfall
d. climate change

6 What can be inferred about the savanna's dry season?

a. It causes animals to travel south to the rainforest.
b. Farmers cannot support their crops during this time.
c. It is growing longer every year.
d. There may be brief periods of rainfall.

7 What makes the Sahel a "transitional" zone?

8 What affects the landscape of the rainforest?

9 What is the vegetation like in the rainforest zone?

Summary

Step 1 **Read the passage again and complete the outline with the words below.**

dry / transitional / farmers / south / climate / savanna
Sahel / vegetation / rainforest / water / trees / crops

I. The Sahel zone

A. A ______________ region between the Sahara and the ______________

B. The driest of the three ______________ zones of West and Central Africa

II. The savanna zone

A. Located ______________ of the Sahel

B. ______________ for part of the year but receives much rain during the rainy season

C. Capable of supporting more vegetation than the ______________

III. The ______________ zone

A. Located south of the savanna

B. Covered in forests with tall ______________ growing close together

C. Gets the most rain of the three zones and has a lot of ______________

IV. The effect of climate on people

A. The Sahel becomes drier every year, so ______________ is hard to find

B. ______________ in the savanna depend on seasonal rains

C. There is little space for ______________ in the rainforest

Step 2 **Complete the summary with your own words based on the outline.**

The Sahel is a ____________ region between the Sahara and the ____________. ____

____

____

____

____

____

______________ There is little space for ______________________ in the rainforest.

Unit 3: How Light Works

Getting Started

1 Look at the picture. Why do you think cities have so many lights?

2 Have you ever seen a rainbow? What colors appeared in it?

3 Why is the sky blue during the day, but black at night?

Building Background Knowledge

Newton's Prism Experiment

In 1665, Isaac Newton conducted an experiment by covering up all the windows in his room, except for one small hole. This allowed a single beam of light to enter. He then put a glass prism in front of the hole, and watched as the white light was turned into a spectrum of rainbow colors. He thought all these colors must be contained within the sunlight. To test this, he placed a second prism upside-down in front of the first. As he guessed, the colors merged back into white sunlight. This proved that white light is actually made up of all the colors of the spectrum.

▲ A beam of white light divided into various colors by a prism

UNIT 3

How Light Works

The Big Question

How does light help us see the world?

▸ Notes

Imagine yourself in your bedroom at night. There are no lights on, so everything is dark, but then you turn on your desk lamp and light fills the room. Suddenly, you can see your desk, your bed, your closet, and everything else in your room. This is because light allows us to perceive the shape and color of the objects in our world.

But what is light, and how does it do this? Light is a type of **energy** emitted by different **sources**. Most of the light on Earth is created by the sun. However, things like fire and desk lamps also give off light. The light they create travels outward like a **wave**, similar to when you throw a small rock into a pond. Yet, waves of light travel much, much faster than waves in a pond.

When you look at a light source, you can see it because its light waves travel directly to your eyes. But most objects do not create light. We see them because light **bounces off** the objects and then enters our eyes. We call this bouncing a **reflection**. When light is reflected from an object to our eyes, our brain analyzes the reflection in order to determine the shape of the object. This is how light enables us to see things around us.

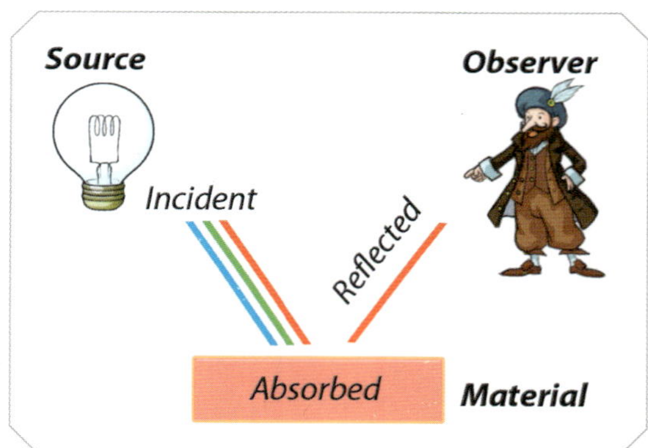

▲ The process of reflection

The reflection of light also lets us see color. White light, like sunlight,

energy the capacity that something has to work, move or bring about change
source the beginning, or the starting point, of something
wave a line that rises and falls
bounce off to move away from a surface as the result of striking it

▸ Notes

is a combination of different waves, and each wave represents a specific color. We notice these colors when sunlight shines through a **prism**, a special piece of glass that bends each wave differently, so the colors separate. Together, the individual colors that make up white light are called the **spectrum**.

When light bounces off an object, not all the light waves are reflected to your eyes. Some of them are absorbed by the object. The other waves are reflected, and they determine the object's color. For example, a red apple only reflects red light, and a leaf only reflects green light. Black objects, like **coal**, don't reflect any light, but rather absorb all the light waves.

Think back to your dark bedroom. When you turn on your lamp, light waves immediately travel from the light bulb in all directions. The waves reflect off your desk, your bed, and your closet. Then, your eyes and brain use these reflections to see the shape and color of each object.

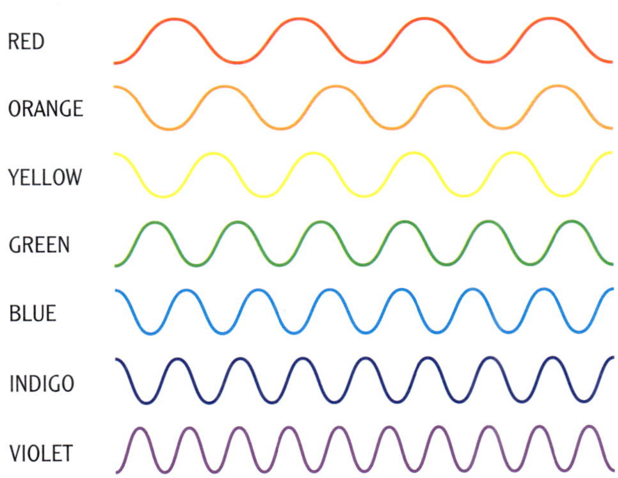

▲ Light travels in waves, and each color has a different wavelength. The longest wavelength belongs to red, and the shortest to violet.

On Your Own

What is one thing you see when you turn on the light in your room? Describe its shape and color.

reflection the action of light or sound changing direction as a result of bouncing off a surface

prism a transparent block of glass that can divide white light into different colors

spectrum the range of colors in white light, visible when separated by a prism

coal a black, dense matter that can be burned as fuel

Vocabulary Building

[1-5] Complete each sentence with one of the words from the box.

object / absorb / separate / analyze / direction

1. The dog ran toward a shiny ______________ on the beach.

2. The children ran in the ______________ of the ball.

3. It is a bad idea to ______________ baby animals from their mothers.

4. If there is more rain falling than the ground can ______________, a flood may occur.

5. The scientists were able to ______________ the graph and use it to make predictions.

[6-10] Choose the words that are closest in meaning to the underlined ones.

6. Although no one spoke, I could <u>perceive</u> extreme tension in the room.

a. doubt b. sense c. mention d. triumph

7. I love this painting because of the <u>combination</u> of colors.

a. spark b. festival c. mixture d. creation

8. The inverted v-shapes on the map <u>represent</u> mountains.

a. symbolize b. detail c. challenge d. decide

9. I wish I had a magic car that would transport me to work <u>immediately</u>.

a. instantly b. gradually c. naturally d. virtually

10. In order to stay together, the tour group cannot take <u>individual</u> sightseeing requests.

a. universal b. rare c. uniform d. personal

[11-13] Complete each sentence with the following idioms.

turn on / **give off** / **make up**

11. Volcanoes can ___________________ gases, steam and ash.

12. The ingredients that ___________________ this dish are expensive and hard to find.

13. As soon as I got home, I ___________________ the television to watch the news.

Reading Comprehension

1 What is the main idea of the passage?

a. Each light wave represents a specific color.
b. Light enables us to see the world around us.
c. The ideas of color and light are different.
d. Our brain and eyes work together to see light.

2 What happens when light waves are reflected?

a. They bounce off an object.
b. They change an object's shape.
c. They pass through an object.
d. They block an object's color.

3 What type of light is reflected by a leaf?

a. green light
b. red light
c. orange light
d. all types

4 The word emitted in the passage is closest in meaning to

a. built up
b. carried
c. sent out
d. touched

5 According to the passage, which of the following is NOT true about sunlight?

a. It represents most of the light we see on Earth.
b. It travels at very fast speeds.
c. It contains all colors.
d. It is completely absorbed by white objects.

6 What can be inferred about the colors in the spectrum of white light?

a. We cannot see them unless they pass through or reflect off an object.
b. They do not really exist until the light is bent by a prism.
c. The number of colors depends on the strength of the light source.
d. Some of them can be eliminated by shining the light through glass.

7 Why does every object have a specific color?

8 What are some examples of light sources?

9 How is your brain involved in the process of using light to see?

Summary

Step 1 **Read the passage again and complete the outline with the words below.**

energy / light wave / directions / objects / sources / waves
shapes / spectrum / reflect / bounces off / absorb / enters

I. Light is a kind of ____________

A. It is created by different ____________ and travels in ____________

II. Light is reflected by objects

A. It ____________ things before entering our eyes

B. The reflections show us the ____________ of objects

III. Each color is a specific kind of ____________

A. White light is made up of a(n) ____________ of different colors

B. Objects ____________ some waves, and those they ____________ make the color we see

IV. How light works in a bedroom

A. It travels from a lamp in all ____________

B. The light reflected off objects in a room ____________ our eyes and allows us to see the ____________

Step 2 **Complete the summary with your own words based on the outline.**

Light is a kind of ____________ that is created by different ____________ and travels in ____________. ____

____

____

____

____

____ The light reflected off objects in a room ____________ our eyes and allows us to see the ____________.

Unit 4: The Food Chain

Getting Started

1. Look at the picture. What is happening?
2. What do you think it means when a relationship between a number of people or things is referred to as a "chain"?
3. What are some basic things humans need to survive?

Building Background Knowledge

Photosynthesis

Photosynthesis is a process used by green plants to create sugar that can be used for energy. But what is used to make this sugar? The main ingredient is light energy, which comes from sunlight. Other ingredients include water, which the plant's roots extract from the soil; carbon dioxide, which is a chemical compound found in the air; and chlorophyll, which is naturally found in the plant's cells. This chlorophyll first absorbs the light energy from sunlight. It then uses it to separate the water's hydrogen molecules from its oxygen molecules. When the hydrogen is joined with carbon dioxide, a kind of simple sugar is created.

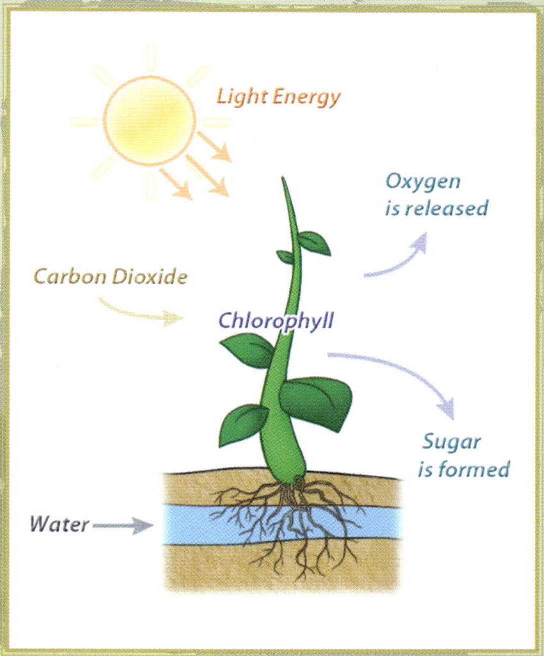

UNIT 4

The Big Question

What does a food chain mainly describe?

The Food Chain

05

► Notes

Food chains describe how all creatures on our planet rely on one another as sources of food. At the base of most food chains there are **producers** like green plants and other **organisms**. They produce food in a process called photosynthesis, capturing the sun's energy and storing it in their cells as sugars. This energy is then passed from creature to creature up the food chain.

Organisms that cannot make their own food depend on other living things to sustain them and are called **consumers**. There are different levels of consumers; primary consumers include plant-eating animals like mice. Known as herbivores, they eat only producers and do not consume other animals. These primary consumers are themselves consumed by meat-eating animals, or carnivores, referred to as secondary consumers. Cats are secondary consumers, since they eat mice. In some food chains, there are tertiary or third-level consumers. A wolf that eats both cats and mice would be a tertiary consumer. Secondary and tertiary consumers that eat plants in addition to animals, such as pigs, cows, and bears, are called omnivores.

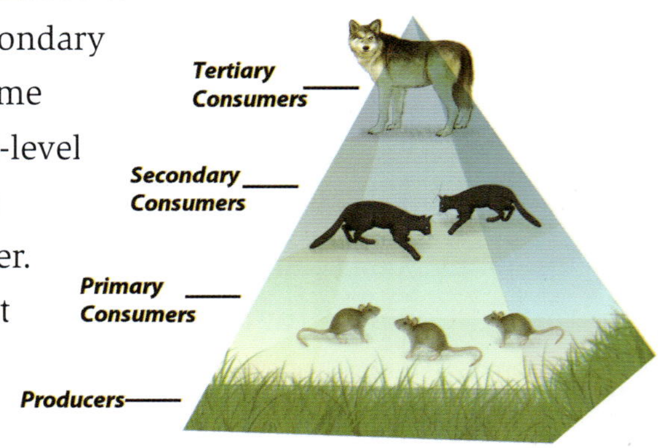

▲ Energy pyramid

The food chain does not end with tertiary consumers. After being transferred from producers to consumers, the

producer a living thing (like a plant) that makes its own food and can be used for food

organism a living thing

consumer a living thing that must eat other living things as food in order to live

decomposer a living thing that consumes and breaks apart dead matter

energy in a food chain moves to **decomposers**. These are organisms like **bacteria** and **fungi** that break down dead **tissues** and return nutrients to the soil to feed the growth of new producers. Thus, the food chain's energy continues to be exchanged.

One way to visualize the energy within a food chain is as a pyramid with a wide base and narrow top. Only about 10% of the energy an organism receives through consumption is transferred to the level above. The rest is used by the organisms for maintenance and movement, or is lost as body heat. Consequently, the total amount of energy in the pyramid is constantly decreasing as it rises through the different levels of consumers.

Each food chain shows only one of the many possible **paths** that can carry the sun's energy from producers to consumers to decomposers. In nature, individual food chains are connected in a network that is referred to as a food web. Food webs demonstrate the many different paths by which an organism may both find food and feed others. Looking at Earth's creatures in this light shows how we are all linked in the natural cycle of life and death.

► Notes

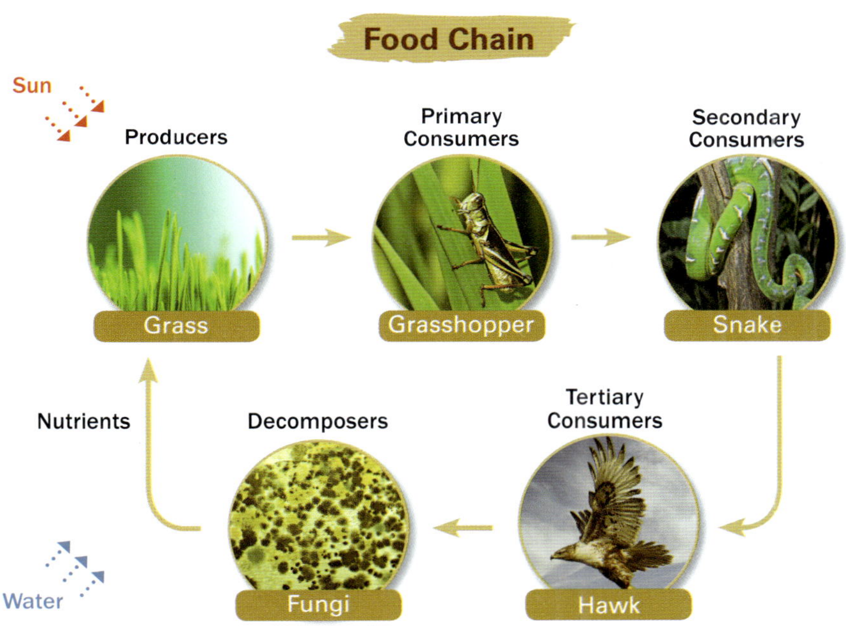

On Your Own

Describe the food chain for one item of food you ate today.

bacterium[*pl.* bacteria] a very small living thing which often causes a disease

fungus[*pl.* fungi] a living thing that consumes decaying matter

tissue a group of cells that form parts of living things

path a course along which some process occurs

Vocabulary Building

[1-5] Complete each sentence with one of the words from the box.

sustain / transfer / nutrients / visualize / demonstrate

1. Many parts of the Sahara desert are too dry to ______________ vegetation.

2. The engineer will ______________ how to use the machine in front of the class.

3. A body that does not get proper ______________ over a long time becomes unhealthy.

4. Students were encouraged to ______________ the diagram in their minds before drawing it.

5. If you ______________ to a school in another city, be sure to let me know.

[6-10] Choose the words that are closest in meaning to the underlined ones.

6. The old house is beautiful, but the <u>maintenance</u> of the grounds is very expensive.

a. upkeep b. furniture c. nurturing d. balancing

7. <u>Primary</u> school prepares students for secondary school.

a. supplementary b. positive c. final d. initial

8. The buildings of the capital are <u>connected</u> by underground tunnels.

a. joined b. separated c. corrected d. displayed

9. Every <u>creature</u> on the planet would die without oxygen.

a. waterway b. collection c. organism d. mammal

10. I can't get any work done because they are <u>constantly</u> making noise next door.

a. honestly b. quickly c. temporarily d. continually

[11-13] Complete each sentence with the following idioms.

depend on / in addition to / break down

11. ____________________ being talented, an Olympic athlete must be dedicated.

12. In order to live on their own, children have to be taught not to ____________________ their parents.

13. Over many hundreds of years, the stone walls have begun to ____________________.

Reading Comprehension

1 What is the main idea of the passage?

a. Food chains show how organisms rely on each other for food.
b. Much energy is lost as it moves up the food chain.
c. Consumers are divided into groups based on what they consume.
d. Energy from the sun is the source of all life on Earth.

2 What is shown in a pyramid-shaped food chain?

a. the ways in which energy is expended by an organism
b. the many food chains to which a single organism belongs
c. the differences between omnivores and carnivores
d. the quantity of energy that is transferred from level to level

3 What role do decomposers play in the food chain?

a. They help plants perform photosynthesis.
b. They serve as food sources for omnivores.
c. They return energy to the soil.
d. They turn sunlight into energy.

4 The word network in the passage is closest in meaning to

a. result　　b. system
c. display　　d. form

5 Which of the following is NOT true of plants?

a. They are able to "feed" on energy from the sun.
b. They depend on consumers for food.
c. They store food energy within themselves.
d. They are eaten by various consumers.

6 What can be inferred about tertiary consumers?

a. They can survive on less food than other consumers.
b. They must consume more food than primary consumers.
c. They have fewer predators than secondary consumers.
d. They are more often omnivores than carnivores.

7 Where does the energy in all food chains originate?

8 What is an herbivore?

9 What is a food web?

Summary

Step 1 **Read the passage again and complete the outline with the words below.**

becomes / bottom / carnivores / energy / herbivores / soil
process / pyramid / omnivores / rely on / photosynthesis / web

I. **Food chain**

A. Describes how ____________ is passed from creature to creature

II. **Producers**

A. Make up the ____________ of the food chain

B. Turn light from the sun into sugars through ____________

III. **Consumers**

A. ____________ other organisms for food

B. Differentiated by what they consume (____________ eat only plants, ____________ eat only animals, ____________ eat both)

IV. **Decomposers**

A. ____________ dead matter and return energy to the ____________

V. **Different ways to visualize the food chain**

A. As a(n) ____________ showing decreasing energy moving up the chain

B. As a(n) ____________ showing all the ways an animal finds food and ____________ food

Step 2 **Complete the summary with your own words based on the outline.**

The food chain describes how ____________ is passed from creature to creature. ________

____

____

____

____

____

A food ________ shows all the ways an animal finds food and ________ food for others.

Unit 5: Pancakes of the World

Getting Started

1. What do you see in the pictures? What are their similarities and differences?
2. What is your favorite kind of pancake topping or filling? What other kinds would you like to try?
3. Is there any food from your country that is also loved in other parts of the world? If so, what is it?

Building Background Knowledge

Pancake Day

Pancake Day, or Shrove Tuesday, is the day before the beginning of Lent–the forty-day period before Easter when Christians traditionally moderate themselves to show their devotion to God. In the old days, rich foods were strictly banned during this period, so families would try to eat up all their eggs, sugar and butter the day before. Pancakes were found to be a good way to use up these ingredients, and they eventually became the traditional dish associated with Shrove Tuesday. Today in England everyone celebrates Pancake Day. There are pancake races, in which people run while holding a frying pan and flipping a pancake. There are also pancake tossing contests, in which contestants must try to toss a pancake as many times as they can in a minute.

▲ People tossing pancakes during a Pancake Day celebration in England

UNIT 5

Pancakes of the World

06

The Big Question

In what ways do the world's pancakes differ?

▸ Notes

Pancakes exist as both a meal and a snack food in many parts of the world. Ancient pancakes were more like bread, made with flour and water. Today's pancakes are more nutritious. Their **recipes** can include a wide variety of ingredients depending on where they're made and who makes them.

The characteristically thick, circular pancakes of North America are famous worldwide. There are numerous recipes for this traditional breakfast food but most call for flour, eggs, milk, baking powder, and sugar. They are generally accompanied by maple syrup and butter. However, they can also be served with an assortment of **toppings** such as chocolate chips, fresh fruit, or powdered sugar.

Crepes, French pancakes, are much thinner than those of North America. Nonetheless, they are comparable in terms of ingredients, lacking only baking powder. Sweet crepes are served as a dessert or snack and may be topped with anything from sugar or syrup to fruit or chocolate. On the other hand, **savory** varieties are main-course meals made with **buckwheat** flour. They feature fillings like cheese, ham, and vegetables.

▲ Dosa

The thin, crispy dosa is the Indian version of a pancake. It is flat and wide, and instead of incorporating flour, milk, and eggs, dosa **batter** is made from rice and ground black **lentils**. Often

recipe instructions for making a certain food
topping something you put on top of food to make it look good or to add flavor
savory tasty, but not sweet
buckwheat a small grain used for making flour

► Notes

stuffed with meats and vegetables, dosas are typically served with a curry dish. They may sometimes be considered a breakfast food but are also eaten at other times of day.

The consumption of pancakes has been closely tied to religious rituals in some countries. In England, it was once customary to eat pancakes on Shrove Tuesday. This custom eventually led to the annual tradition of Pancake Day. Today, British people of all religions enjoy eating pancakes and holding festive competitions like pancake tossing on Pancake Day.

If you would like to make pancakes of your own, try this simple recipe for pikelets, the pancakes of Australia.

Ingredients:
1 egg
1/4 cup sugar
1/2 cup milk
1 cup self-raising flour

1) **Whisk** together the egg, sugar, and milk.
2) Slowly add flour and stir the batter until it is smooth.
3) Pour a spoonful of batter onto a greased frying pan over medium heat.
4) When the top bubbles, flip the pancake with a **spatula** and cook it until both sides are golden brown.
5) Top the pancakes with honey, jam, or maple syrup.

▲ Pikelets

On Your Own

What type of pancake introduced in the passage would you like to try most? Why?

batter a mixture that usually contains flour and milk or water and is used for cooking
lentil a small bean-like seed that can be eaten
whisk to mix quickly so that air is added
spatula a flat kitchen tool mostly used to turn things over while cooking

Vocabulary Building

[1-5] Complete each sentence with one of the words from the box.

customary / rituals / competition / stir / ingredient

1. My brother won a photography ______________ last month.

2. Pour some milk into the coffee and ______________ it with a spoon.

3. The cake is not delicious because I left out an important ______________.

4. In Spain, it is ______________ to eat dinner relatively late.

5. The ______________ involved in weddings differ from country to country.

[6-10] Choose the words that are closest in meaning to the underlined ones.

6. Their jobs are <u>comparable</u> in that they both work with the public.

a. limiting b. different c. likable d. similar

7. Our <u>annual</u> awards ceremony was cancelled this year due to a funding shortage.

a. yearly b. famous c. excessive d. probable

8. Our team's problem is that we <u>lack</u> confidence.

a. miss b. explore c. seek d. help

9. Specialty shops offer a wider <u>assortment</u> of imported cheeses than local markets.

a. match b. variety c. value d. style

10. I'm not rich by any means, but I have some money <u>nonetheless</u>.

a. anytime b. even c. still d. moreover

[11-13] Complete each sentence with the following idioms.

in terms of / call for / be accompanied by

11. This kind of problem ____________________ hard work and cooperation.

12. Young children must ____________________ an adult on some of the rides.

13. Alaska, ____________________ area, is the largest state in the United States.

Reading Comprehension

1 What is the main idea of the passage?

a. The most common type of pancake is found in North America.
b. Some pancakes are healthier than others.
c. Most types of pancakes share the same batter recipe.
d. Pancakes appear in different forms all over the world.

2 What is true about pancakes in England?

a. There is a special day named after them.
b. They are thin, crispy, flat, and wide.
c. They are only eaten on Tuesdays.
d. People eat them only at religious events.

3 How should flour be added to pikelet batter?

a. by stirring it quickly with a spatula
b. by warming it first in a frying pan
c. by mixing it in a little at a time
d. by whisking it together with the eggs

4 The word stuffed in the passage is closest in meaning to

a. served b. filled
c. cooked d. seen

5 Which of the following is NOT true of the Indian dosa?

a. It is eaten along with a dish featuring curry.
b. It is thin and wide and has a crispy texture.
c. It is served at various times of the day.
d. Its batter is similar to that of other pancakes.

6 What can be inferred about different varieties of pancakes?

a. They are generally considered to be a breakfast food.
b. They originally held a religious significance.
c. They originated from North America.
d. Dosas are generally savory rather than sweet.

7 What were the earliest pancakes like?

8 Which pancake is best known around the world, and what is it like?

9 How do savory crepes differ from sweet crepes?

Summary

Step 1 **Read the passage again and complete the outline with the words below.**

annual / circular / England / earliest / rice / vary
modern / nutritious / sweet / pikelets / Indian / thin

I. The ______________ pancakes

A. Were more like bread than pancakes today

II. ______________ pancakes

A. More ______________ than the original pancakes

B. ______________ by location in batter ingredients, toppings and fillings

III. Different pancakes of the world

A. North American pancakes: thick and ______________, famous, served with butter or syrup

B. French crepes: ______________, either ______________ or savory

C. ______________ dosas: made with ______________ and lentils, served with curry

D. Pancakes in ______________: connected to a religious ritual, focus of a(n) ______________ celebration

IV. Recipe for making pancakes

A. Australian ______________ are simple to make and are served with sweet toppings

Step 2 **Complete the summary with your own words based on the outline.**

The ____________ pancakes were more like bread than pancakes today. ________________

____

____

____

____

____

____ If you like pancakes,

Australian ____________ are simple to make and are served with sweet toppings.

Unit 6: The Children of Ancient Rome

Getting Started

1. Look at the picture. Do you know what country it is from? If so, what things do you know about the country?
2. What is your daily routine like? Describe it.
3. Think of the jobs and roles that men and women have. Are they the same or are they different?

Building Background Knowledge

Ancient Rome

Ancient Rome was once a small agricultural settlement. Back in 753 B.C., the city of Rome was founded in what is now central Italy. Over the course of centuries, Roman civilization grew from a kingdom to a republic to an empire. Eventually the Roman Empire grew so big that it was split into two halves—the Western Roman Empire (Europe and North Africa) and the Eastern Roman Empire (Turkey and parts of Asia). Due to political troubles and constant foreign attacks, the Western Roman Empire finally fell in the year 476, but the Eastern Roman Empire survived for another thousand years. Ancient Rome contributed greatly to the development of the Western world, and its history still influences modern society.

▲ The Roman Empire at its greatest extent in 117

UNIT 6

The Big Question

What were kids' lives like in ancient Rome?

The Children of Ancient Rome

07

► Notes

In ancient Rome, when a baby was born, families observed a simple birth ceremony to mark the occasion. According to custom, the infant was placed before the father who then picked it up to symbolically accept the baby into the family.

Once they got a bit older, Roman children spent their leisure time socializing, playing games, and having fun. Pets were common, including typical animals like dogs, as well as some that might seem unusual today, like pigeons, geese, and monkeys! Just like modern kids, Roman kids loved playing with toys. Parents provided their children with **stilts**, kites, marbles, and the ankle bones of a sheep, which were used to play a traditional game called **knucklebones**. Roman youth played other games too, such as tic-tac-toe and board games, in addition to war games, which were especially popular among boys.

The clothing worn by Roman kids was not very similar to the fashions we wear now. They typically wore a kind of dress known as a toga, which was made out of a long, **draping** piece of material wrapped across the body. In addition, boys and girls wore a piece of jewelry called a *bulla*, a necklace that was supposed to protect them during childhood.

▲ Roman clothing

stilt one of two wooden sticks that has a place for the foot and is used to raise a walking person

knucklebones an ancient game played with five small objects which are thrown up and caught

drape to cause cloth to hang or fold over something

locket a piece of jewelry with a small space for holding things, generally worn around the neck on a chain

It included a **locket** that held special **charms** to ward off evil.

▸ Notes

In Rome's earliest days, a child's education was the responsibility of his or her parents. Boys learned to read and write, and girls learned to **sew** and **weave**. Eventually, formal schools were created and some children began to receive education outside the home. However, schooling was not free, and many families could not afford to send their children to be formally educated. At school, children of wealthy parents were instructed in basic subjects like reading, writing, and math. Many girls, though, did not receive any schooling at all. At 12 or 13, boys from wealthy families studied Latin and Greek grammar and **literature**. At 16, they had the opportunity to study public speaking, which was a very important skill for Romans.

When kids grew up, their opportunities were highly influenced by their gender. Men typically worked outside the home, while women were usually confined to managing the house and household finances. They were not allowed to hold government positions, or to be lawyers or teachers. Those careers were only for wealthy men who had received a special education when they were younger.

▲ Roman statue of a girl playing knucklebones

On Your Own

Which subjects did you learn when you first began school?

charm a small object designed to protect its owner, often worn on a necklace or bracelet
sew to join together with needle and thread
weave to use an interlacing pattern to make clothing or baskets
literature artful and expressive writing

Vocabulary Building

[1-5] Complete each sentence with one of the words from the box.

socialize / typical / observe / accept / formal

1. The ceremony for swearing in a president is very ____________.

2. Everyone in this group must ____________ the rules no matter what.

3. A(n) ____________ pizza is topped with tomato sauce and cheese.

4. If both universities ____________ you, which one will you attend?

5. I was in the same class as my husband at school, but we didn't ____________.

[6-10] Choose the words that are closest in meaning to the underlined ones.

6. You can have a dog, but walking and feeding it will be your <u>responsibility</u>.

a. duty b. merit c. invention d. pleasure

7. To celebrate the <u>occasion</u>, we had a party in the garden.

a. history b. event c. victory d. statue

8. Does the price <u>include</u> the service charge?

a. lack b. comprise c. remove d. limit

9. The company will <u>provide</u> the money to build the new art center.

a. claim b. supply c. perfect d. collect

10. It is the supervisor's responsibility to <u>manage</u> all the team projects.

a. adjust b. abandon c. afford d. control

[11-13] Complete each sentence with the following idioms.

ward off / be supposed to / according to

11. The pizza at this restaurant ________________ be the best in town.

12. The boy was last seen hiking on a trail near the canyon, ________________ reports.

13. It is said that throwing salt over one shoulder will ________________ bad luck.

Reading Comprehension

1 What is the main idea of the passage?

a. The gender roles of ancient Rome are out of date by modern standards.
b. Kids growing up in ancient Rome were not as happy as modern kids.
c. There are similarities and differences between ancient Roman kids and modern kids.
d. Education in ancient Rome influenced the development of modern education systems.

2 In what way were Roman women and Roman men from poor families alike?

a. They could not be government officials, lawyers, or teachers.
b. They only had the opportunity to study basic subjects.
c. They were educated by tutors instead of going to school.
d. They worked within the home rather than outside of it.

3 According to the passage, how was a *bulla* worn?

a. hanging from the neck
b. draped across the shoulder
c. as a layer over a toga
d. wrapped around the waist

4 The word finances in the passage is closest in meaning to

a. family members
b. economics
c. rules
d. chores

5 Which of the following is NOT mentioned in the passage as a pastime of Roman kids?

a. playing with stilts, marbles, and kites
b. competing at tic-tac-toe or board games
c. going to the theater together
d. pretending to fight in battles

6 What can be inferred about wealthy Roman men?

a. They owned more than one home.
b. They most often chose to become educators.
c. They were sometimes expected to speak in public.
d. They were named as government officials at an early age.

7 How did Roman education change over time?

8 What did Roman families do to celebrate the birth of a child?

9 What roles did boys and girls have when they grew up?

Summary

Step 1 **Read the passage again and complete the outline with the words below.**

bulla / toga / girls / father / games / pets
formal / managed / outside / wealthy / accepted / poor

I. Babies in ancient Rome

A. Were ceremoniously ______________ into the family by the ______________

II. Kids' pastimes and clothing of ancient Rome

A. Played ______________, had toys, and kept ______________

B. Wore a(n) ______________ for clothing and a necklace called a(n) ______________

III. Kids' education in ancient Rome

A. ______________ families were able to pay to send children to ______________ schools

B. ______________ children and many ______________ did not receive an education

IV. When kids grew up

A. Women ______________ the house and worked within the home

B. Educated men worked ______________ the home in specialized careers

Step 2 **Complete the summary with your own words based on the outline.**

When a baby was born in ancient Rome, it was ceremoniously ___________ into the family by the ___________. ____

____

____

____

____

____

____ Conversely, educated men worked ___________ the home in specialized careers.

Part II

• Content Area : Culture

Unit 7: National Flags of the World

Getting Started

1. Look at the picture. What colors and shapes do you see?
2. What does the flag of your country look like?
3. What symbols can represent a country?

Building Background Knowledge

Material and Nonmaterial Culture Traits of a Society

Every country has its own culture, a complex and unique blend of various cultural traits. Some of these cultural traits are material, meaning they are things which can be held or touched. Examples of material cultural traits are clothes, toys, buildings, food, artwork, and machines. They are the kinds of things which we immediately notice as being different when we travel abroad. Other cultural traits are nonmaterial, and they include such things as customs, political systems, ceremonies, language, and religion. Forms of greeting, such as shaking hands, kissing, or bowing, are also examples of nonmaterial culture traits. Of course, nonmaterial aspects of a culture can be expressed through material items. For example, a country's ideas and beliefs might be expressed through its national flag.

▲ The Sphinx and Chephren Pyramid in Giza, Egypt

▲ The Great Wall of China

▲ Symbols for world religions

UNIT 7

The Big Question

How do national flags convey meaning?

National Flags of the World 08

► Notes

A national flag is a flag that symbolizes national **identity**. It stands for a country's land, its **population**, and its government. The colors or shapes on a country's flag often express beliefs that are important to the citizens of the country.

One of the most important features of a national flag is its color. While a certain color may symbolize the same concept among different nations, it can also vary. On the Chinese and Vietnamese flags, for instance, the color red stands for **revolution**, while its appearance on the Albanian and Peruvian flags represents **hardiness** and blood respectively. The color blue symbolizes the sky on the Argentinian and European Union flags, and the sea on the flag of Greece. In an expression of cultural **solidarity**, many Arab nations fly flags that feature the colors green, red, white, and black.

The meaning of a national flag may also be expressed through shapes. The star, for example, often represents the unity of the individual groups or states that came together to form a country, as in the flag of the United States. Another shape with a widely recognized meaning is that of the star and **crescent**, which in many Muslim nations stands for peace and life, important beliefs in Islam. Similarly, the shape of the cross, symbolic of **Christianity**, is featured on the national flags of a number of Christian nations. Of course, there are also shapes whose meanings are not global,

identity the qualities that make a person or group what they are

population a group of living organisms that share certain traits

revolution a sudden, complete change in government

hardiness the quality of being able to withstand difficulties

but rather specific to individual countries. For example, the sword on the flag of Saudi Arabia represents justice, while the crossed swords on the flag of Guatemala symbolize honor.

Many combinations of color and shape are possible, but some countries have flags that are almost identical. Such similarities may result from shared **origins**, or they can simply be coincidence, as in the case of Indonesia and Monaco. Both countries fly a flag that is divided horizontally, with the top half red and the bottom white. For the people of Indonesia, the flag stands for courage and purity of intent. In Monaco, the flag represents the traditional colors of the Grimaldi family, which has ruled the nation since the 13th century.

The next time you look at a national flag, try to determine what symbolic meaning it has, for this will give you a glimpse into the country, its culture, and its people.

► Notes

▲ Flag of Peru

▲ Flag of Argentina

▲ Flag of Turkey

▲ Flag of Saudi Arabia

On Your Own

What symbols does your country's flag have?

solidarity agreement between all the members in a group, resulting from their shared beliefs

crescent the shape of the moon when less than half of it is visible

Christianity a religion based on the teachings of Jesus Christ

origin where something comes from

Vocabulary Building

[1-5] Complete each sentence with one of the words from the box.

identical / honor / unity / respectively / vary

1. Cameras ______________ in price and quality, and a high price does not necessarily mean high quality.

2. We loved that toaster so when it broke, we bought a(n) ____________ one.

3. Though Mongolia is a vast country, ______________ among the people exists.

4. The nation thanked the hero for his ______________ and bravery.

5. My sisters Kimberly and Doris are 15 and 17 years old ______________.

[6-10] Choose the words that are closest in meaning to the underlined ones.

6. The tune is so different when played by the violinist that you'll hardly <u>recognize</u> it.

a. hum b. know c. practice d. appreciate

7. The science fiction film gave them a <u>glimpse</u> into what life might be like in the future.

a. glance b. sensitivity c. temptation d. misbelief

8. The director was unhappy when the cast misunderstood his <u>intent</u>.

a. purpose b. outcome c. guilt d. innocence

9. It was only by <u>coincidence</u> that we met, since neither of us planned on going out.

a. plan b. mistake c. experience d. chance

10. You can manipulate this clay to <u>form</u> nearly any shape you wish.

a. apply b. view c. make d. cross

[11-13] Complete each sentence with the following idioms.

stand for / for instance / result from

11. The snake in that painting ___________________ forces of evil.

12. There are many serious illnesses that can ___________________ smoking.

13. Camels, ___________________, are an example of an animal that has uniquely evolved.

Reading Comprehension

1 What is the main idea of the passage?

a. Color is a more powerful symbol for flags than shape.
b. Countries with similar flags have a similar history.
c. The design of a nation's flag tells a lot about the country.
d. Governments use national flags to unite people.

2 How do some Christian nations demonstrate their shared religious values?

a. by including the same shape on their flags
b. by giving their flags the same dimensions
c. by flying flags with similar color schemes
d. by making their flags exactly the same

3 What is true about Indonesia and Monaco?

a. Both of their flags were designed by the same person.
b. Their flags are similar, but not because of their cultures.
c. Their royal families are distantly related.
d. Red stands for courage in both of the countries.

4 The word specific in the passage is closest in meaning to

a. valuable
b. unique
c. important
d. formal

5 Which shape is NOT mentioned in the passage as expressing the same meaning on multiple flags?

a. the sword
b. the cross
c. the star
d. the crescent

6 What can be inferred about Greece?

a. The color blue represents the power of its leaders.
b. Its flag is one of very few that features the color blue.
c. It has no cultural ties to Argentina or the European Union.
d. The sea is an important part of the culture of its people.

7 Which concepts are represented by a national flag?

8 Why do Arab nations use similar colors on their flags?

9 How is the meaning of the color red different for different countries' flags?

Summary

Step 1 **Read the passage again and complete the outline with the words below.**

beliefs / colors / identity / expressed / meanings / global
origins / shapes / different / coincidence / similarities / crescent

I. The symbolism of national flags

A. Represent the ____________ of a nation

B. Important ____________ of citizens are ____________ through colors and shapes

II. ____________ on national flags

A. Can have similar or different ____________ on different flags

B. Similar colors may show ____________ in culture among countries

III. ____________ on national flags

A. Shapes like the star, ____________ and cross have ____________ meanings

B. Shapes like the sword can mean ____________ things on different flags

IV. Similar-looking national flags

A. May result from shared ____________ or can be a ____________

Step 2 **Complete the summary with your own words based on the outline.**

National flags represent the ____________ of a nation. ________________________________

____

____

____

____

____

____ Flags that look very similar to each other can be the result of the countries' shared ____________ or it may be a ____________.

Part II

• Content Area : Physical Science

Unit 8: Sound and Echolocation

Getting Started

1. Do you have a favorite sound? What kind of sounds do you dislike?
2. Hearing is one of our five senses. Do you know the other four?
3. What do you think makes it possible for bats to hunt for food?

Building Background Knowledge

The Hearing Organ

Sounds are all around us, and our ears are the organs responsible for hearing them. Our ears actually have three parts: the outer, middle, and inner ears. The outer ear, which is the part we can see, is designed to gather outside sounds and direct them toward your middle ear. Your middle ear is then used to transport these sounds to your inner ear, which interprets them and sends special messages to your brain that explain what they are. And your ears aren't just used for hearing—they also help you keep your balance. This is why people with an ear infection sometimes complain of dizziness.

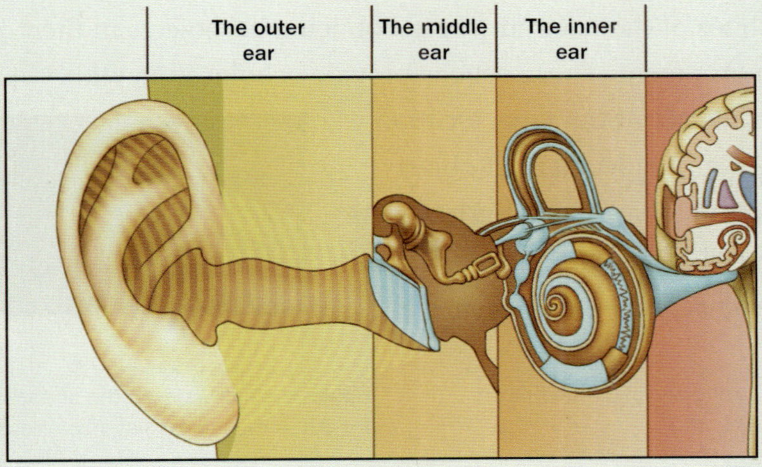

UNIT 8

Sound and Echolocation

The Big Question

How does echolocation work?

▸ Notes

Since it is invisible to our eyes, sound is something that is hard to picture. It is a form of energy that is made by **vibrations**. Imagine tapping two spoons together. The spoons vibrate, causing nearby **particles** of air to move. These moving particles of air cause other particles of air to move too, just like **ripples** of water. These movements, which we call sound waves, travel away from their source, the spoons. Eventually they reach your ear and you hear the ringing sound the spoons produced.

Our bodies have the amazing ability to receive and make sense of these vibrations in the air. When sound waves arrive at your ear, the information gets passed along until it reaches your brain. The brain can determine what made the sound and where it came from.

Some organisms, including bats, dolphins, whales, and even specially trained humans, can do even more with sound waves. They use sound to sense their environment through an ability called echolocation. First, echolocators emit sound waves. Then they listen for the echoes of their sound waves bouncing off objects in their environment. These echoes provide echolocators with details about the type, location, size, and movement of objects around them. The **length** of time an echo takes to return indicates distance, while changes in the

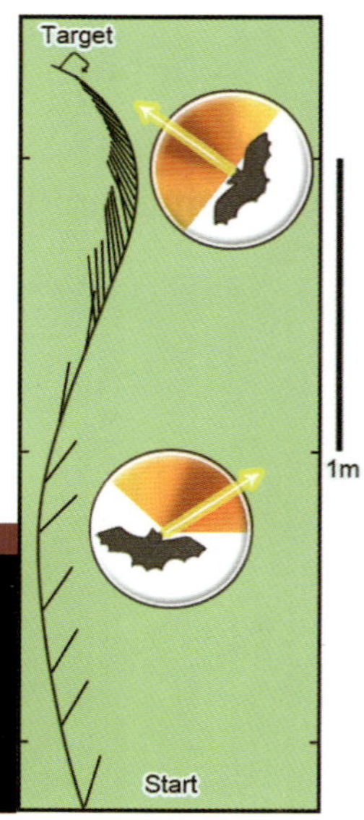

The sound beam of a bat seen, from overhead, as the bat searches for, identifies, and catches an insect ▸

vibration repetitive shaking while staying in one place
particle a tiny piece of matter
ripple a small wave on the surface of water
length a measured distance or duration

sound of an echo provide information about size and **texture**.

► Notes

Echolocation allows organisms to navigate and hunt in complete darkness, so it is ideal for nocturnal animals. Nocturnal animals are those that are active at night, like bats. Bats are probably the world's best-known echolocators. When bats use echolocation, they make **ultrasound** noises, which are too high-pitched for human ears to hear.

Bats' ability to use echolocation is so effective that they can "hear" a wire that is just 0.08 millimeters wide. They can also hear the difference between things they might want to eat and other less interesting objects in their environment. In other words, they know whether they have located a delicious **moth** or a dried leaf. Once a moth has been found using echolocation, the bat grabs the **prey** in its mouth. Some species of moths have the ability to hear bats' ultrasound and can escape before they become food.

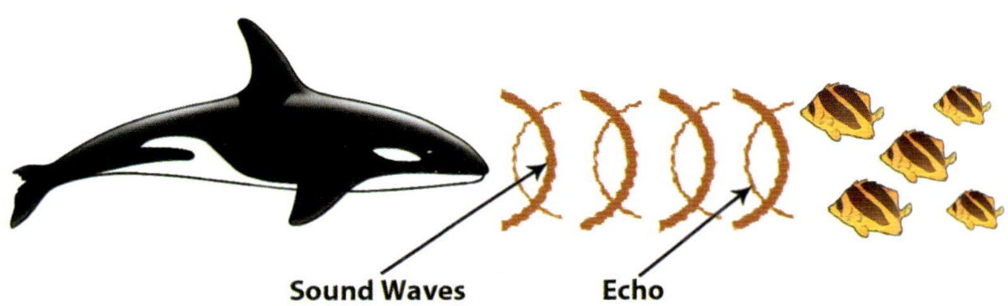

▲ The sound waves from a whale's song traveling forward and returning as an echo

On Your Own

What kinds of sounds make your daily life more convenient?

texture the way the surface of something appears to the eyes and to the touch

ultrasound sound that is above the range that humans can hear

moth a kind of insect that is similar to a butterfly but duller in color

prey an animal that may be eaten by another animal

Vocabulary Building

[1-5] Complete each sentence with one of the words from the box.

grab / details / invisible / species / navigate

1. Do you remember any ____________ about the house in your dream?

2. This ____________ of bird is known for its unique mating call.

3. The insect that causes the damage is so small that it is almost ____________.

4. The captain was able to ____________ the ship through the rocky waters.

5. Please ____________ that newspaper off the table before the wind blows it away.

[6-10] Choose the words that are closest in meaning to the underlined ones.

6. Giraffes' long necks help them <u>reach</u> the leaves on high branches.

a. beat b. spread c. run for d. stretch to

7. When <u>determining</u> which career is right for you, consider factors other than money.

a. communicating b. questioning c. pardoning d. deciding

8. She worked hard to help her children <u>escape</u> their humble beginnings.

a. destroy b. convince c. conclude d. evade

9. Through <u>effective</u> use of irrigation, the farmers were able to grow crops in the dry land.

a. efficient b. ambitious c. hilarious d. precise

10. I'd like to change seats because the woman behind me keeps <u>tapping</u> her foot against the back of my chair.

a. hitting b. sliding c. brushing d. smacking

[11-13] Complete each sentence with the following idioms.

make sense of / **in other words** / **have the ability to**

11. She ________________ learn languages quickly and easily.

12. I will gladly drive if you help me ________________ the map.

13. I want to be a scientist who makes robots. ________________, I want to be a robotic engineer.

Reading Comprehension

1 What is the passage mainly about?

a. how sound travels through air in the form of a wave
b. methods of navigation among various organisms
c. bats' sense of hearing and use of echolocation
d. sound waves and their use in echolocation

2 How does sound normally travel?

a. It moves away from its source in wave-like vibrations of air particles.
b. It slows the movement of air particles until they reach our ears.
c. It produces particles that travel outward from the source.
d. Its waves echo off of different objects before entering our ears.

3 What is true about the noises bats make when they use echolocation?

a. They go unnoticed by humans.
b. They are used for communication with other bats.
c. They can travel farther than most noises.
d. They differ depending on whether it is day or night.

4 The word indicates in the passage is closest in meaning to

a. finds
b. decreases
c. shows
d. moves

5 Which of the following is NOT true about bats?

a. They are more active during the night than during the day.
b. They have better eyesight than non-nocturnal animals.
c. Their echolocation can identify minute objects.
d. They sometimes feed on insects such as moths.

6 What can be inferred about bats' prey?

a. They try to hide by mimicking a dried leaf.
b. Some cannot detect the noises of hunting bats.
c. The majority is made up of moth species.
d. Most of them communicate with ultrasound.

7 How does our sense of hearing work?

8 What information does echolocation provide the organisms that use it?

9 Why is echolocation beneficial for nocturnal animals?

Summary

Step 1 **Read the passage again and complete the outline with the words below.**

ripples / location / echoes / information / objects / tiny
nocturnal / ultrasound / vibrations / navigate / accurate / brain

I. What is sound?

A. A kind of energy produced by ______________

B. A wave that travels through air like ______________ of water

C. Processed by the ______________ to give ______________ about our surroundings

II. Sound and echolocation

A. Echolocators make sounds and listen for ______________ bouncing off ______________

B. The echoes provide details about the ______________, size, and movement of objects

C. Useful for ______________ animals like bats

III. Bats' use of echolocation

A. ______________ noises help bats ______________ and hunt in the dark

B. Their echolocation is very ______________ and can detect ______________ objects

Step 2 **Complete the summary with your own words based on the outline.**

Sound is a kind of energy that is produced by ______________ and travels through the air in waves like ______________ in water. ____

____

____

____

____

____

Their echolocation is very ______________ and can detect even ______________ objects.

Unit 9: The Human Immune System

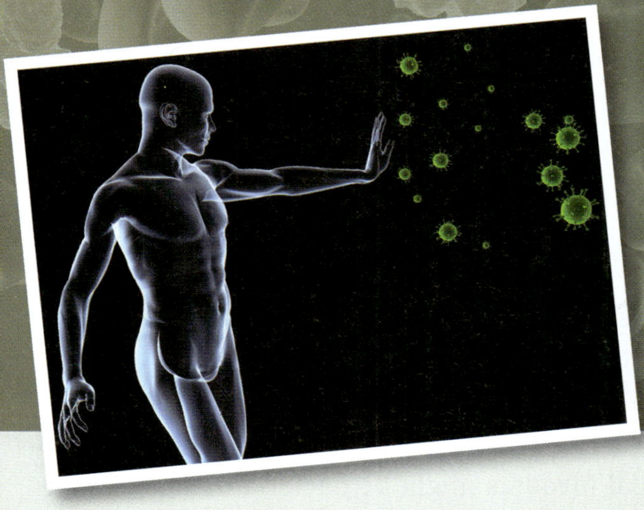

Getting Started

1. What causes people to get sick?
2. Have you been sick recently? How long did it take you to get better?
3. How do you think your body fights sickness?

Building Background Knowledge

Bacteria and Infection

Bacteria are one-celled organisms that can be found nearly everywhere, both inside and outside of our bodies. They are among the oldest and most numerous creatures that exist on earth, but they are so small that they generally cannot be seen without a microscope. Most of the bacteria that enter our bodies are stopped from doing any harm by our immune systems, and some of them can even have beneficial effects. But sometimes, such as when they enter the body through a cut in the skin, they will cause an infection. These infections are characterized by redness, swelling, and pain.

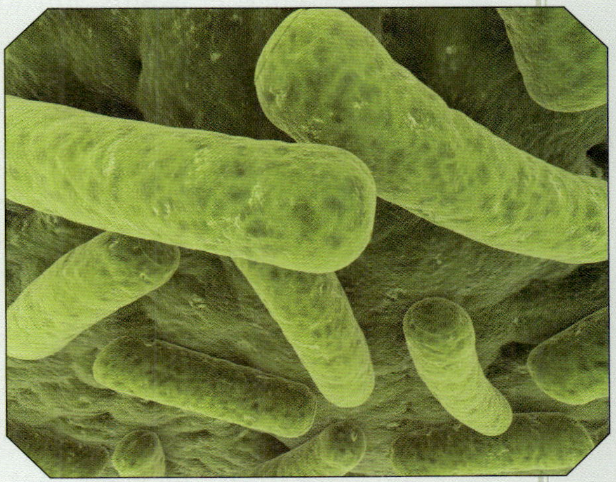

▲ Bacteria

UNIT 9

The Human Immune System

The Big Question

What is the purpose of the immune system?

► Notes

The human body is like a castle that can defend itself against invaders. For the human body, typical invaders might be bacteria that can cause **infections** or diseases. We call our body's defenses the "immune system." We rely on this system to keep us healthy by finding, attacking, and destroying germs that make us sick. There are many different kinds of germs in the world, but luckily the immune system has numerous ways to fight them off.

The immune system's first line of defense is external: our skin, nose, eyes, and mouth. Our skin covers most of our body, so it forms a physical barrier against intruders, but it also provides the body with advance warning about invading germs. In addition, the skin makes **antibacterial** substances, or chemicals that kill bacteria. Of course, there are places our skin does not cover, such as our eyes, nose, and mouth. There, other substances obstruct germs in much the same way as the skin does on the rest of the body. Moreover, the sticky **mucus** in your nose and mouth contains **enzymes** capable of destroying bacteria, as do the saliva and tears produced by your mouth and eyes.

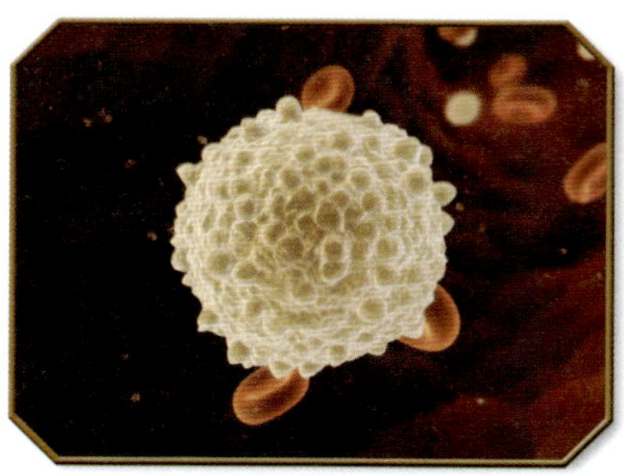

▲ White blood cell

In the event that the body's external defenses fail to repel a foreign object, the inside of the body has other ways of protecting against invaders. White

infection the invasion of the body by germs
antibacterial fighting or stopping the growth of bacteria
mucus a slippery bodily fluid
enzyme a chemical substance produced by living cells that contributes to important chemical reactions in the body

► Notes

blood cells are the key players in our internal defense. These cells come in several different types, which work together to detect and combat germs. Some **digest** invasive germs and others aid in recollection and recognition of germs the body has previously encountered. Additionally, certain types of white blood cells possess special tools known as **antibodies** to respond to invaders. Different antibodies correspond to different germs. When they find a matching germ, they attach to it like a key fitting into a keyhole. The antibody then locks up the germ to prevent it from doing damage inside the body.

Although most of the immune system's actions are carried out without our knowing, it is sometimes possible to tell that our defenses are functioning properly and working to keep us healthy. Perhaps you have experienced **swelling** of your neck's **lymph glands** when you had a sore throat. Or maybe you cut your finger and watched it heal within a matter of days. If so, you have witnessed your immune system reacting to and battling infection.

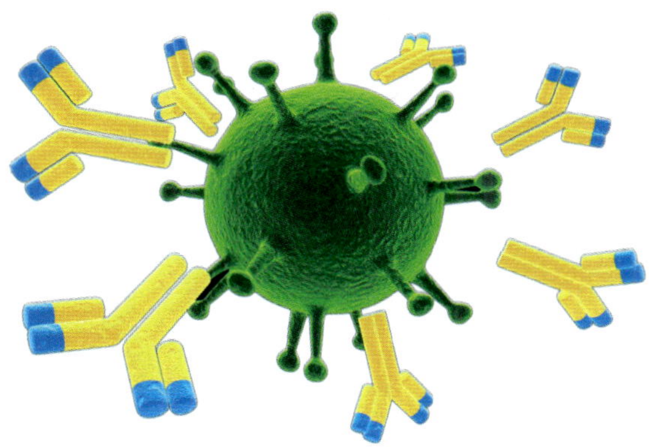

▲ Antibodies attacking a virus

On Your Own

Do you think your immune system is working well? Why or why not?

digest to change food into energy and waste

antibody any of various substances in the body that fights infection

swelling an instance in which a part of the body becomes larger

lymph gland(node) a tissue mass in the body that helps fight infection by catching foreign particles

Vocabulary Building

[1-5] Complete each sentence with one of the words from the box.

germ / invaders / recognition / substance / recollection

1. The Great Wall of China was constructed to keep ______________ out.

2. Scientists have researched the ______________ that causes the disease.

3. Our children have no ______________ of the town we used to live in.

4. Diamonds are the hardest ______________ known to exist.

5. The employees were unhappy because they did not receive ______________ for their hard work.

[6-10] Choose the words that are closest in meaning to the underlined ones.

6. If you <u>witness</u> a crime, it is your responsibility to report it.

a. assist b. observe c. promote d. request

7. A dog's ears can <u>detect</u> sounds that a human's ears cannot.

a. magnify b. crawl c. perceive d. nourish

8. Despite the power failure, the hospital continued to <u>function</u> normally.

a. earn b. succeed c. benefit d. operate

9. During a solar eclipse, you can watch the moon <u>obstruct</u> the light of the sun.

a. block b. reflect c. intensify d. diminish

10. If you're going to be late, please give us <u>advance</u> notice.

a. progressive b. unlimited c. prior d. eventual

[11-13] Complete each sentence with the following idioms.

fight off / lock up / carry out

11. If you eat well and get enough sleep, your body can more easily ____________________ infection.

12. Let me ____________________ my house, and then we can leave.

13. In order to ____________________ the plan, we will need five volunteers.

Reading Comprehension

1 What is the passage mainly about?

a. how to treat an infection by germs
b. how our immune system keeps us healthy
c. how white blood cells attack invaders
d. how bacteria affect our bodies

2 Why are antibodies described as keys?

a. They lock out germs to keep them from entering the body.
b. Each one fits into a particular type of germ.
c. They are the most important players in the immune system.
d. Each one is responsible for a different part of the body.

3 What is the purpose of the enzymes in mucus, saliva, and tears?

a. to help white blood cells work
b. to kill bacteria before they enter the body
c. to alert the body that it has an infection
d. to physically obstruct germs from entering the body

4 The word combat in the passage is closest in meaning to

a. battle
b. reach
c. press
d. define

5 Which of the following is NOT mentioned as a tool the body uses to handle germs?

a. chemicals in the skin
b. white blood cells with antibodies
c. swelling of the eyes, nose, and mouth
d. mucus in the nose and mouth

6 What can be inferred about the immune system's external defenses?

a. They depend on our skin in order to function.
b. We are usually aware when they are active.
c. They do not keep out all harmful invaders.
d. Mucus is the key component of each of them.

7 Why is the body compared to a castle at the beginning of the passage?

8 What are some signs that your immune system is working?

9 What three things does the skin do as part of the immune system?

Summary

Step 1 **Read the passage again and complete the outline with the words below.**

heals / kills / warns / knowing / lock / recover
identifying / germs / mucus / skin / effects / mouth

I. The immune system

A. Protects the body from infection by ____________

II. External defenses

A. The ____________ keeps out germs, ____________ the body, and also ____________ some germs

B. ____________, saliva, and tears in the nose, ____________, and eyes block or kill germs

III. Internal defenses

A. White blood cells combat germs by ____________ and digesting them

B. Antibodies correspond to specific germs and ____________ them up

IV. ____________ of the immune system

A. Works all the time without us ____________

B. We can tell it is working when it ____________ cuts and helps us ____________ from illnesses

Step 2 **Complete the summary with your own words based on the outline.**

Our immune system protects our body from infection by ____________ with external and internal defenses. ____

____

____

____

____

______________________________ However, we can tell the immune system is working when it ____________ our cuts and helps us ____________ from illnesses.

Unit 10: The Ancient Olympic Games

Getting Started

1. Do you know where and when the Olympic Games first began?
2. Do you like playing sports? How can they be helpful to young people?
3. Do you enjoy watching the Olympics? Why or why not?

Building Background Knowledge

Ancient Greece

Ancient Greece was a civilization which flourished during the period from 1100 B.C. to 146 B.C. It was one of the most powerful empires of its time. In the eighth century B.C., ancient Greece consisted of numerous city-states, each with their own individual laws and leaders. However, the ancient Greeks were still united by a shared language and religion. Over centuries, their culture developed many new ideas in the fields of art, science, government, and philosophy. Although they were eventually conquered by the Romans, the Greeks had a strong influence on the Roman Empire, and together, the two cultures formed the basis of much of Western civilization.

UNIT 10

The Ancient Olympic Games

The Big Question

What role did the Olympics play in ancient Greek society?

▸ Notes

Our modern Olympic Games are based on a much older tradition that was practiced by the ancient Greeks, beginning in 776 B.C. **Athletic** competition was only part of the early Olympics; their primary function was to honor the Greek gods. The games were held once every four years in a village on the Greek coast called Olympia.

At this time, Greece was made up of hundreds of independent city-states that often fought wars against one another. However, the Olympics were considered more important than political differences, existing as a reminder of a shared culture. For this reason, the games were always preceded by a month-long "**sacred truce**." During the truce, all city-states had to stop their wars, no matter how tense the fighting. Moreover, each had to offer safe passage through its territory to athletes and **spectators** traveling to the Olympics.

The citizens who journeyed to Olympia were mostly men. Women were not allowed to compete in the games, and married women were even barred from entering as spectators. Athletes generally competed naked, unless the rules of their sport required them to don special equipment.

There were nine events in the ancient Olympics. One was the footrace, which included two short-distance **sprints** and one long-distance run. In the **chariot** race, **contestants** competed in horse-drawn carts. Boxing, wrestling, and a mixture of the two called pankration were the toughest events, as there were few rules to keep contestants from injuring each other. There were two throwing events: javelin and discus. In the former,

athletic having to do with sports
sacred truce a highly special and respected agreement to stop fighting for a perid of time
spectator a person who watches an event or game
sprint a (usually) short run at the highest speed possible

athletes threw a **spear** at a target for accuracy, while in the latter a heavy bronze disc was thrown for distance. Competitors attempted to jump as far as they could in the jumping event. And finally, the pentathlon was a combination of five other events: discus, javelin, running, wrestling, and jumping.

▲ These drawings represent some of the sports played at the ancient Greek Olympics.

► Notes

Olympic activities lasted five days, two of which were allotted for religious ceremonies and three for the actual games. In addition to their religious significance, the games were seen by the Greeks as a celebration of courage and the beauty of the human form. Winning athletes were awarded **laurel wreaths** and other prizes and were regarded as heroes by all Greeks.

▲ A column at the Temple of Zeus, built by the ancient Greeks in Olympia

On Your Own

What is your favorite event in the Olympics?

chariot an ancient wagon with two wheels that was drawn by a horse

contestant a person who competes in a contest

spear a weapon with a sharp end attached to a long stick

laurel wreath a circle of leaves or branches that symbolizes victory, and was worn by the winner of a competition

Vocabulary Building

[1-5] Complete each sentence with one of the words from the box.

accuracy / practiced / allot / reminder / significance

1. This special ceremony has been ______________ every year since 1750.

2. This e-mail is a(n) ______________ to those who will be attending the health fair.

3. You should ______________ some time for exercise when creating your schedule.

4. The battle's ______________ was not understood until many years later.

5. Contestants will be judged on the speed and ______________ of their performance.

[6-10] Choose the words that are closest in meaning to the underlined ones.

6. A dispute over <u>territory</u> started the war.

a. region b. ambition c. difference d. charity

7. Justin <u>attempted</u> to escape through a window.

a. hesitated b. prepared c. tried d. achieved

8. The local people are very proud that their country remains <u>independent</u>.

a. merciful b. courageous c. powerful d. self-governing

9. Mike was <u>barred</u> from membership to the club.

a. blocked b. urged c. ordered d. arrested

10. After many failures, the nation has come to <u>regard</u> the president as a disappointment.

a. view b. overestimate c. imagine d. ignore

[11-13] Complete each sentence with the following idioms.

be based on / be made up of / be preceded by

11. The team will ____________________ some experienced players and some new ones.

12. The banquet will ____________________ an address from a surprise guest speaker.

13. Many holiday traditions ____________________ beliefs and practices of the past.

Reading Comprehension

1 What is the main idea of the passage?

a. Olympia is where the first Olympics were held and it gave the games their name.
b. The ancient Olympics mixed religious ceremony with athletic competition.
c. The Olympics in ancient Greece were used to train soldiers for battle.
d. Each of the nine events in the ancient Olympics had a different religious meaning.

2 What was the purpose of the "sacred truce"?

a. to allow warring peoples to participate in the games
b. to remind Greeks of their honored gods
c. to make sure the city of Olympia was not attacked
d. to give city-states a chance to resolve their arguments

3 What was true of the footrace event?

a. Women were allowed to compete in it.
b. It included three different races.
c. Runners also participated in the chariot races.
d. It was the most important Olympic event.

4 The word don in the passage is closest in meaning to

a. show b. put on
c. hold onto d. leave

5 Which ancient Olympic event did NOT involve the throwing of an object?

a. javelin b. pentathlon
c. pankration d. discus

6 What can be inferred about the city-states of ancient Greece?

a. Each contributed athletes to the Olympic competitions.
b. None of them had total authority over ancient Greece.
c. They would join forces to fight against non-Greeks.
d. Each possessed a different cultural history.

7 Why were the ancient Olympics considered more important than the city-states' political differences?

8 What were the nine events featured during the ancient Olympics?

9 What did winning Olympic athletes receive?

Summary

Step 1 **Read the passage again and complete the outline with the words below.**

athletes / heroes / four / nine / Olympia / gods
courage / common / at war / before / participate / form

I. The ancient Olympics

A. Held every ______________ years in ______________ starting in 776 B.C.

B. Main purpose was to honor the Greek ______________

II. Ancient Greek city-states

A. There were hundreds, and they often were ______________

B. They shared a(n) ______________ culture

C. A "sacred truce" was called ______________ the games so everyone could ______________

III. At the games

A. ______________ and most spectators were men

B. ______________ different events were held

C. Competitions were seen as a celebration of ______________ and the human ______________

D. Winners received prizes and were treated like ______________

Step 2 **Complete the summary with your own words based on the outline.**

Held every ______________ years in ______________, Greece, the main purpose of the Olympics was to honor the Greek ___________. ______________________________

____

____

____

____

____

________ Winners received prizes and were treated like ______________ by all Greeks.

Part III

Unit 11: Medieval Castles

Getting Started

1. Have you ever seen a castle in a movie or on TV? Describe how it looked.
2. What do you think medieval castles were mainly used for?
3. There are various kinds of houses around the world. What kind of house would you most like to live in?

Building Background Knowledge

Feudalism

Feudalism was a system of governance that began in France around 900 A.D., spreading throughout Europe over the next 150 years. The system was established when kings and queens began to lose control of their centralized kingdoms. They started giving control of local areas to the lords that lived there. The lords were given ownership of the land, as well as the peasants that lived there and all of their possessions. In return for this power, the lords pledged to be loyal to the king and queen, and to send knights to protect them when necessary. Meanwhile, the peasants were forced to work for the lords, farming their land and performing whatever tasks were required.

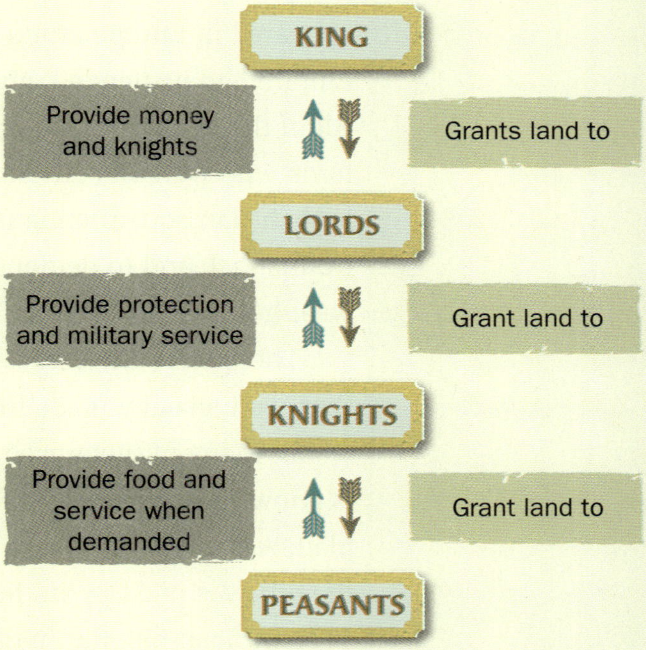

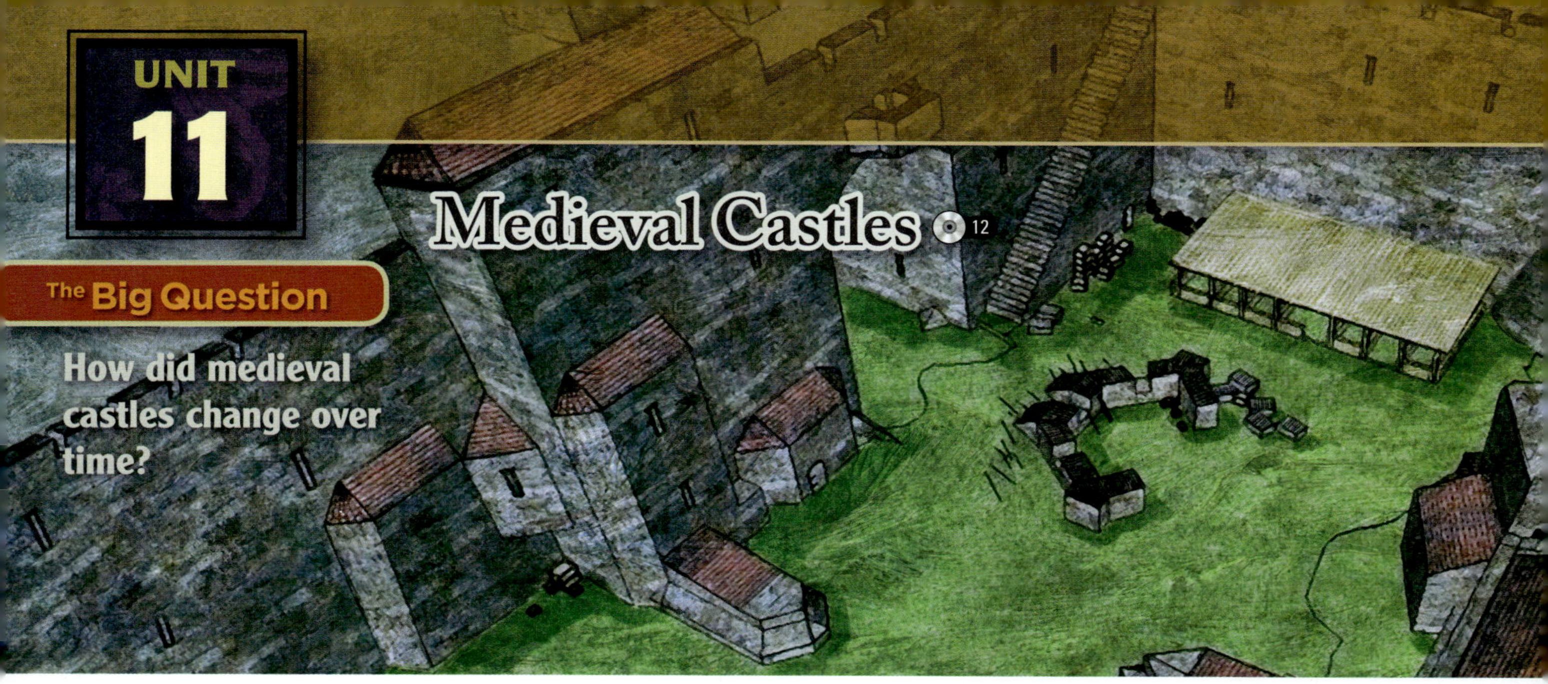

UNIT 11

Medieval Castles

The Big Question

How did medieval castles change over time?

▸ Notes

Based on what we see in the movies, castles seem very romantic and elegant. They are common in love stories, fairy tales, and legends about princesses; but in real life castles were not always so ideal. Most early castles, for example, were cold, dark, and wet. Besides that, the air was smoky from open fires, **pests** were a common problem, and there was no **plumbing**.

Castles evolved from basic **fortified** camps, which were widely built in Roman times and perhaps even earlier. Castles as we think of them first appeared in Europe around the 9th and 10th centuries A.D. The Carolingian Empire had just ended, giving rise to what is known as a feudal society. All of the empire's territory was divided up and controlled by individual lords who were in constant competition with each other. The lords began constructing forts both to protect their land from attack and to demonstrate their power and wealth.

These were the earliest castles, and they were usually made from wood. Many of them used what is known as a "motte-and-bailey" plan. A circular **ditch** was dug and the dirt was piled up in the middle. This artificial hill–the "motte"–was where the castle was built. The

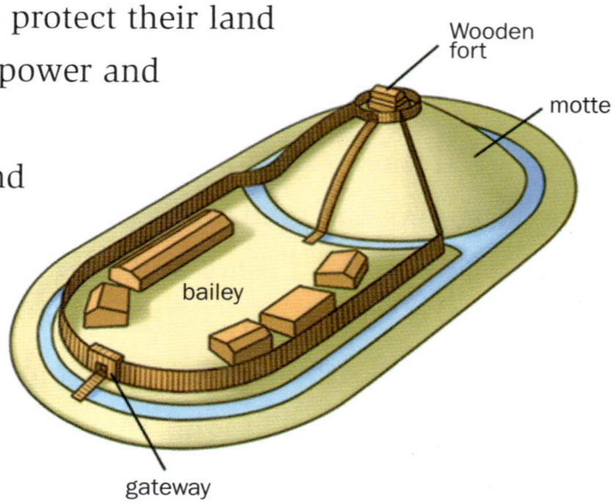

▲ Motte-and-bailey

pest an insect or animal that is harmful to humans
plumbing a system of drains and pipes that bring in and take away water and gas
fortify to make something stronger in order to protect it
ditch a long, narrow channel that is dug into the ground, usually as a way to direct water or divide land

"bailey" was a surrounding area protected by a heavy wooden fence. Over time, castles gradually changed, growing larger and taller, and wood construction was replaced by stone. Later castles featured towers, giant walls, and new defensive systems. As they advanced, castle architecture improved as well, and many examples of elaborate and beautiful castles can still be seen in Europe today.

▸ Notes

At first, life inside castles was uncomfortable. They were awful places to live in because they were cold and dark and could not even keep out the wind. There were no bedrooms, so people slept on benches or simple mattresses in the castle's halls. Eventually, sleeping chambers were built inside castles, making them more comfortable. Fireplaces provided heat, and candles provided light. Castles were beginning to transform into more than just defensive military structures. In time, people built chapels, prisons, **armories**, government offices, and **treasure houses** within the castle walls. They also created ponds, wells, **orchards**, and gardens. At their best, castles were like cities, where people went about their daily lives. Huge feasts, exciting **tournaments**, and weddings were all part of castle life in later centuries.

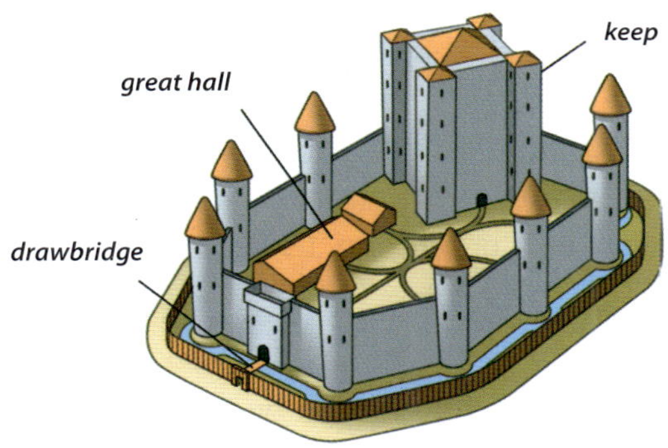

▲ Stone keep castle

On Your Own

How is your house different from a medieval castle?

armory a place where an army's weapons are kept
treasure house a place where valuables are kept and protected
orchard an area where fruit or nut trees have been planted
tournament a competition in which players compete against each other in a series of games until there is one winner

Vocabulary Building

[1-5] Complete each sentence with one of the words from the box.

evolve / architecture / construct / besides / eventually

1. What other music do you like ______________ hip-hop?

2. They predict that the event will ______________ into a multimedia festival.

3. ______________ often reflects the climate conditions of a location.

4. What we throw away today could ______________ harm our descendants.

5. The city has a plan to ______________ a new stadium in the same location.

[6-10] Choose the words that are closest in meaning to the underlined ones.

6. Ten guards are standing outside the king's chambers.

a. lands b. rooms c. neighbors d. lawmakers

7. The countryside surrounding the city is hilly and dry.

a. wasting b. across c. locating d. encircling

8. The structure is made of stone that could not have come from nearby.

a. building b. station c. jewels d. joint

9. It is an artificial lake that was created in 1972.

a. man-made b. imaginary c. enthusiastic d. appropriate

10. Thanksgiving is a feast of thanks enjoyed by family members and close friends.

a. competition b. banquet c. ritual d. fast

[11-13] Complete each sentence with the following idioms.

give rise to / go about / be replaced by

11. The civilizations that ____________________ the Mayan culture left few written records.

12. It was a typical Monday and the workers were ____________________ their business as usual.

13. The old wood cabins have ____________________ a new brick dormitory.

Reading Comprehension

1 What is the main idea of the passage?

a. Stories about castles do not show them as they were in real life.
b. Castles evolved from basic structures to impressive complexes.
c. European medieval castles benefited from building techniques from abroad.
d. Few people lived in castles because conditions inside them were not comfortable.

2 Why were castles first built?

a. to improve living conditions in cities
b. to defend the Carolingian Empire
c. to provide protection for a lord's land
d. to try out new construction techniques

3 What two features are part of the motte-and-bailey plan?

a. a pond and a garden
b. a wall and a tower
c. a ditch and a gate
d. a hill and a fence

4 The word elaborate in the passage is closest in meaning to

a. neat
b. similar
c. old
d. fancy

5 Which of the following is NOT true of castles in later centuries?

a. Most people shared sleeping space in the hallways.
b. They hosted magnificent parties and other events.
c. People grew plants within their walls.
d. They were usually constructed of stone.

6 What can be inferred about castles in fairytales?

a. They are not an accurate reflection of the earliest castles.
b. They are not consistent with the motte-and-bailey design.
c. They do not serve a defensive purpose.
d. They do not feature fireplaces or plumbing.

7 What was European society like in the 9th and 10th centuries?

8 What were some features in later castles that made life more comfortable?

9 How were later castles like "cities"?

Summary

Step 1 **Read the passage again and complete the outline with the words below.**

cities / events / forts / land / heat / commonly
cold / romantic / private / stone / improved / uncomfortable

I. The truth about early castles

A. Not as ______________ as they are in stories

B. Problems like ______________, dampness, smoke, and pests made life ______________

II. Castle evolution

A. Lords first built wooden ______________ to protect their ______________ and show their wealth

B. Motte-and-bailey plan ______________ used in early castles

C. Later castles were bigger, more beautiful, and made out of ______________

III. Life in castles

A. Later castles ______________ living conditions with ______________, light, and ______________ rooms

B. Eventually, castles became like small ______________ with lots of people and ______________

Step 2 **Complete the summary with your own words based on the outline.**

The truth about early castles is that they were not as ___________ as they are in stories.
____
____
____
____
____
____ Eventually, castles became like small ___________ with lots of people living in them and many ___________ being held.

Part III

• Content Area : Economics

Unit 12: How the Stock Market Works

Getting Started

1. What do you usually spend your allowance on?
2. Have you ever heard the terms "stock" or "stock market"? Do you know what they mean?
3. What are the names of some famous companies in your country?

Building Background Knowledge

Corporations

Corporations are quite unlike businesses that are owned by a single person or a partnership. Instead, they are owned by shareholders, who purchase shares of the corporation's stock on the stock market, making them part-owners. Shareholders meet regularly to vote for a board of directors, who then have the power to set company policies, as well as to hire and fire the people who actually run the corporation. Also, in many ways, corporations are legally considered to be individuals. Just like real people, they can own property, make contracts, and file lawsuits. However, when a corporation is sued, its owners are not usually responsible. Even if a corporation fails, the owners don't suffer any consequences other than losing their investment.

UNIT 12

The Big Question

What does the stock market allow people to do?

How the Stock Market Works

13

Notes

Reports on stocks and the stock market fill the daily economic news, but what do these **terms** mean? A stock is one share of **ownership** in a special type of company called a corporation. Corporations have a legal existence independent of the people who run them, and they can sell ownership shares to investors. These investors become **stockholders**, or shareholders, in the corporation.

▲ Building of the New York Stock Exchange

The stock market represents the collective buying and selling of corporations' shares carried out by investors. Today, some of this trading is done online, but investors also meet in buildings to trade. Most corporations, like Google, Disney, and McDonald's, make stocks available in the stock market. They do this to raise money to expand and improve their business. Selling stock allows them to acquire funds without going into **debt**, as they would if they took out a bank **loan**.

There are potential benefits for buyers of stock as well. As partial owners of the business, they share in any profits. This can happen in different ways. The corporation may pay each stockholder a yearly share of its earnings, known as a **dividend**. Or, it might put all its profits into growing the business. While its shareholders will not earn dividends, in theory

term a name used to describe a concept
ownership act of having something as property
stockholder a person who owns shares of a company
debt the state of needing to repay another party

► Notes

the corporation's growth will cause its stock value to rise. Then, if shareholders sell their stocks, they will get more money for them than they paid.

Investors must be wary of stocks, however, for their prices can go down as easily as they can go up. If the corporation performs poorly, its stock value will drop. Not only will shareholders receive no profits, but they will lose money when selling their low-priced shares. Stocks are best seen as a long-term investment. There are no guarantees, but most investors who keep money in stocks for 15 years or more come out ahead.

▲ Real time quotes at a stock exchange

In the short term, stock prices rise and fall according to corporate performance and the trends of the market. When the stock market is increasing in overall value, it is called a "bull market." Similarly, investors who believe stocks will rise and invest **aggressively** are described as "bullish," since bulls are known for charging ahead. Their opposites in economic terms are bears, who are more **cautious** and slow-moving. A "bear market" loses value, just as a "bearish" investor has doubts about the market and invests carefully or even sells off shares.

On Your Own

If you could choose one company to buy stock in, which would it be? Why?

loan money lent with interest charged
dividend a part of a company's profit that is paid to the people with shares in it
aggressively done in a bold way
cautious careful to avoid risks

Vocabulary Building

[1-5] Complete each sentence with one of the words from the box.

investors / available / guarantee / overall / perform

1. The ______________ situation is good, despite a few minor problems.

2. If the company does not ______________ better next year, workers will lose their jobs.

3. Many of the company's ______________ were financially ruined by its bankruptcy.

4. There were still some seats ______________ a few hours before the show.

5. The courier service couldn't ______________ overnight delivery because of the storm.

[6-10] Choose the words that are closest in meaning to the underlined ones.

6. These three countries have become close <u>trading</u> partners.

a. bartering b. changing c. traveling d. joining

7. There was never a <u>doubt</u> that he would become a great musician.

a. belief b. marvel c. uncertainty d. craft

8. How did you come to <u>acquire</u> so many shares of the company?

a. get b. greet c. applaud d. prize

9. Free coffee is one <u>benefit</u> of working in a coffee shop.

a. handicap b. service c. priority d. advantage

10. The airline is hoping to <u>expand</u> its routes to three new countries next year.

a. exaggerate b. increase c. clarify d. degrade

[11-13] Complete each sentence with the following idioms.

in theory / be wary of / come out ahead

11. The company will ____________________ if we just keep working hard on the project.

12. The plan is perfect ____________________ but in reality, it's just not possible.

13. Parents should teach their children to ____________________ strangers.

Reading Comprehension

1 What is the main idea of the passage?

a. Investors must have a solid understanding of the market to make money.
b. Corporations' special legal status enables them to give investors dividends.
c. The stock market usually benefits both corporations and investors.
d. Corporations sell ownership shares to investors who hope to make money.

2 Why do corporations sell stock?

a. to earn funds without acquiring debt
b. to ensure a payoff for their shareholders
c. to limit the power of their founders
d. to be eligible to buy stock in other companies

3 What is a bull market?

a. a market whose average value is decreasing
b. a market whose investors are generally hasty
c. a market whose average value is increasing
d. a market whose investors are generally cautious

4 The word potential in the passage is closest in meaning to

a. usual
b. possible
c. huge
d. attractive

5 Which of the following is NOT true about stocks?

a. They represent partial ownership of a corporation.
b. They can be bought and sold over the Internet.
c. Their value may decrease if their company underperforms.
d. Their value automatically increases after 15 years.

6 What can be inferred about most successful investors?

a. They have been trading stocks for many years.
b. They can be defined as bullish.
c. They invest only in big-name corporations.
d. They do not receive dividends.

7 How is a corporation different from other types of companies?

8 What does a bearish investor do?

9 What are two ways investors can make money in the stock market?

Summary

Step 1 **Read the passage again and complete the outline with the words below.**

companies / corporations / dividends / shares / lose / cautiously
long-term / go down / aggressively / rise / sell / stock market

I. Stocks are shares of ownership

A. Corporations are ____________ with an independent status that can ____________ stock

B. Stocks are bought and sold in the ____________

II. Why stocks are traded

A. ____________ can get money without going into debt

B. Investors can make money by receiving ____________ or selling valuable ____________

III. Investors must be careful

A. Stocks can ____________ in value

B. They should be seen as a(n) ____________ investment

IV. Types of markets and investors

A. Bull markets ____________ in value, and bullish investors act ____________

B. Bear markets ____________ value, and bearish investors act ____________

Step 2 **Complete the summary with your own words based on the outline.**

Stocks are shares of ownership. ____

____

____

____

____

____

____

Conversely, bear markets ____________ value, and bearish investors act ____________.

Unit 13: Sink or Float?

Getting Started

1. What happens to the water level when you get into a bathtub?
2. Name some objects that float in water, and others that don't.
3. Why do you think some objects float in water?

Building Background Knowledge

Archimedes

Archimedes was a famous Greek mathematician, scientist, and inventor. Among his most famous inventions was a device known as the "Archimedes screw," which could transport liquids upward through a tube by means of a revolving screw. But Archimedes is perhaps most famous for his discovery regarding the displacement of water. According to legend, he was asked to find a way to determine if a crown was made of solid gold. It is said that while taking a bath, he realized that if he placed the crown in a tub, it would displace an amount of water equal to its own volume. Excited by his discovery, he is rumored to have run naked through the streets shouting "Eureka!"

UNIT 13

The Big Question

What effect does buoyancy force have on everyday objects?

Sink or Float?

14

► Notes

What happens when you drop an ice cube into a glass of water? The weight of the ice cube pushes away some of the water, and the level of water in the glass rises. But that is not all that happens. The water also pushes upwards against the ice cube. We call this buoyancy force, and it makes some objects **float** in water.

Buoyancy is the opposite of the force of gravity. Gravity pulls an object down towards the earth, while buoyancy pushes it up. If the buoyancy force is greater than gravity, the object floats. When buoyancy is less than gravity, the object **sinks**. To determine which force is greater, we have to compare the **density** of the water with that of the object. Density means how tightly a substance's **molecules** are grouped together.

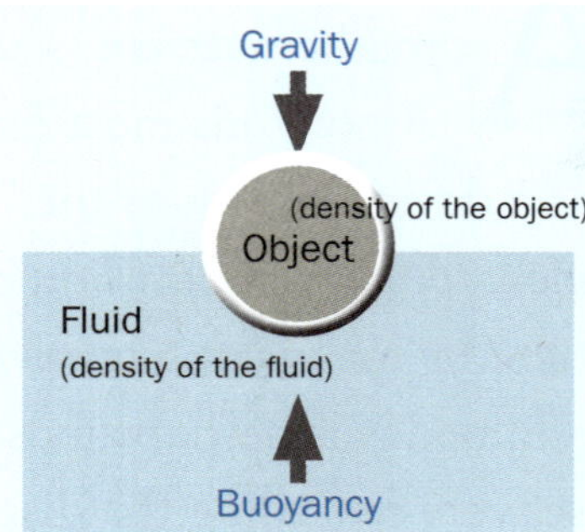

▲ Buoyancy force

The Greek inventor and mathematician Archimedes is famous for being the first to write about buoyancy force. He noticed that when he stepped into the bathtub, the water level in the tub got higher. It was being pushed away, or displaced, by his body. Following this observation, Archimedes performed some **experiments** and came up with the Archimedes Principle. It says that the weight of the water displaced by an object is equal to the weight of the object.

You can see the effects of buoyancy force in a simple experiment. Fill

float to stay at the top of a liquid
sink to drop to the bottom of a liquid
density the amount of matter per unit of space
molecule the smallest unit of a substance that is composed of at least two atoms

▸ Notes

two regular-sized **jars** with **fresh water**, and drop one egg in each jar. Each egg should sink to the bottom, because it is slightly denser than the water. Now, add several tablespoons of salt to jar #1 and stir until it **dissolves**. You should see the egg begin to rise. This happens because salt water is denser than fresh water, giving it a greater buoyancy force with which to push up the egg. Nothing has changed in jar #2: the egg is still denser than the fresh water, so it remains at the bottom.

We can predict whether something will sink or float by examining its density. Metal is very dense, so if you drop a nail into water it will sink. Wood, on the other hand, is not very dense. If you place a block of wood in water, it will float. The buoyancy force of the water is enough to keep the wood from going under.

▲ Salt water (denser)   ▲ Fresh water (less dense)

On Your Own

Which objects in your kitchen do you think will float, and which do you think will sink?

experiment a test done to learn something or to find out if something works or is true
jar a ceramic or glass container, usually used for storing food
fresh water water that is not salty
dissolve to spread out within a liquid

Vocabulary Building

[1-5] Complete each sentence with one of the words from the box.

opposite / compare / determine / bottom / notice

1. The detectives will ______________ the two sets of fingerprints.

2. Did you ______________ that Jack no longer wears glasses?

3. The ______________ of love is hate.

4. There is a small village at the ______________ of the mountain.

5. Only an expert can ______________ whether it is a real bomb or a fake.

[6-10] Choose the words that are closest in meaning to the underlined ones.

6. Is there any way to <u>predict</u> how he will react to the news?

a. theorize b. prevent c. foretell d. advance

7. It's the doctor's <u>observation</u> that the baby's health had improved.

a. finding b. question c. guess d. ignorance

8. These plants are harmful because they <u>displace</u> the plants that naturally grow in the region.

a. force out b. upset c. engage d. exclude

9. If you look closely, you can see that she's <u>slightly</u> taller than her sister.

a. gently b. embarrassingly c. exactly d. somewhat

10. I don't care <u>whether</u> you stay out late tonight or not; just be here on time tomorrow morning.

a. how b. while c. unless d. if

[11-13] Complete each sentence with the following idioms.

come up with / be equal to / on the other hand

11. The idea that we ____________________ for the science fair last year will be hard to top.

12. Imports are increasing; ____________________, exports are decreasing.

13. The pay you'll get ____________________ the amount of work you do.

Reading Comprehension

1 What is the main idea of the passage?

a. Objects that sink in water are not affected by buoyancy force.
b. Buoyancy force is more powerful than the force of gravity.
c. The study of buoyancy began in ancient Greece.
d. Buoyancy force is what makes some items float in water.

2 What is the relationship between buoyancy and gravity?

a. One is caused by the other.
b. They are always equal.
c. They push in opposite directions.
d. Buoyancy is greater than gravity.

3 How can adding salt to water cause an object to float?

a. The density of the water increases.
b. The water becomes warmer.
c. The weight of the object decreases.
d. The object rests on top of the salt.

4 The word remains in the passage is closest in meaning to

a. moves b. rolls
c. stays d. forms

5 According to the passage, which of the following is NOT true about Archimedes?

a. He observed a scientific principle while taking a bath.
b. He conducted an experiment to demonstrate water density.
c. He learned that heavier objects displace more water.
d. He developed a theory related to the weight of displaced water.

6 What can be inferred about the density of ice?

a. It is greater than that of water.
b. It is equal to that of water.
c. It is less than that of water.
d. It changes when in water.

7 What does density describe?

8 What did Archimedes realize when he stepped into the bathtub?

9 Why does a block of wood tend to float when you place it in water?

Summary

Step 1 **Read the passage again and complete the outline with the words below.**

bathtub / water / density / floats / experiment / sink
denser / more / gravity / displaces / pushes up / weight

I. The effects of buoyancy force

A. An ice cube in water ____________ some of the water and ____________

B. The water's buoyancy force ____________ on the object, the opposite of ____________

C. The object's ____________ determines whether it sinks or floats

II. The Greek inventor and mathematician Archimedes

A. Saw water displacement in the ____________

B. Discovered that the ____________ of an object determines how much ____________ it displaces

III. Buoyancy force in the real world

A. A(n) ____________ can show the effects of buoyancy

B. When water is ____________, it pushes on objects with ____________ buoyancy force

C. Objects denser than the water will ____________

Step 2 **Complete the summary with your own words based on the outline.**

An ice cube in water ____________ some of the water, and ____________ because of buoyancy force. ______________________________

____

____

____

____

____

On the other hand, objects that are very dense, like metal, almost always ____________.

Unit 14: How Spacesuits Work

Getting Started

1 Look at the picture. What functions do you think spacesuits have?

2 Why do you think people travel to space?

3 If you could travel beyond our planet, where would you like to go and why?

Building Background Knowledge

A Brief History of Space Travel

Space has always held a special fascination for humans. Our earliest ancestors would gaze at the stars and create stories to explain them. Later, ancient astronomers were able to identify some of our solar system's planets in the night sky. During the Renaissance, astronomers calculated the orbits of these planets around the sun. And in the 17th century, the invention of the telescope led to new discoveries. But it wasn't until after World War II that rocket science allowed us to break free of gravity and launch objects into space. Since then, humans have walked on the moon and unmanned spacecraft have landed on Venus and Mars. Many different human-made vehicles are currently traveling in space, collecting information about the universe.

UNIT 14

The Big Question

Why do astronauts need spacesuits?

How Spacesuits Work

15

▸ Notes

Working in the harsh environment of space, astronauts have unique needs that spacesuits are designed to meet. Within the interior of a spacecraft, the **atmosphere** is strictly regulated, making special clothing unnecessary. However, in space there is little or no **air pressure**. If the human body were exposed to the vacuum of open space, its fluids would be unable to remain in a liquid state and would start to boil. Therefore, spacesuits are designed to create a mobile environment with the right amount of air pressure.

The suits provide astronauts with a breathing supply of pure **oxygen** rather than the mixture of 78% **nitrogen** and 21% oxygen that is found in Earth's atmosphere. Before putting on a suit, the astronaut must eliminate all of the nitrogen from his or her system. Otherwise, bubbles of nitrogen gas may form within body fluids, causing a painful condition known as "the bends." In addition to providing oxygen, the spacesuit deals with the carbon dioxide that astronauts breathe out, which can be dangerous in large amounts. **Canisters** in the spacesuit remove the gas so it does not build up inside the suit and harm the astronaut.

Spacesuits also physically shield astronauts from a barrage of micrometeoroids, small pieces of rock that fly through space at high speeds. These have the potential to cause a great deal of damage, so spacesuits have a sturdy protective layer made out of high-tech materials like those used in body armor. Additionally, spacesuits are designed to control interior temperature. Heating and cooling systems insulate the

atmosphere the mixture of gases that is around a planet
air pressure the force exerted by the weight of air
oxygen a colorless gas that is present in air on Earth and needed for most animals and plants to live
nitrogen a colorless gas that forms most of the Earth's air

astronaut from the severe temperature fluctuations caused by the exposure to or absence of sunlight, which may range from –160 to 120 degrees Celsius.

Another important feature of a spacesuit is its **communication** system. Space missions use **radio equipment** to maintain contact among spacewalking astronauts, their spacecraft, and **ground controllers**. Every spacesuit has a microphone and a pair of earphones in the helmet for communication. By coordinating their actions in this way, astronauts are able to carry out complex activities beyond the safety of their spacecraft.

With each new space mission, spacesuit technologies have been improved. Suit designs will doubtlessly continue to evolve as we learn more about living and working in space. Thanks to the spacesuit, human beings have the capacity to more intimately explore the universe.

▸ Notes

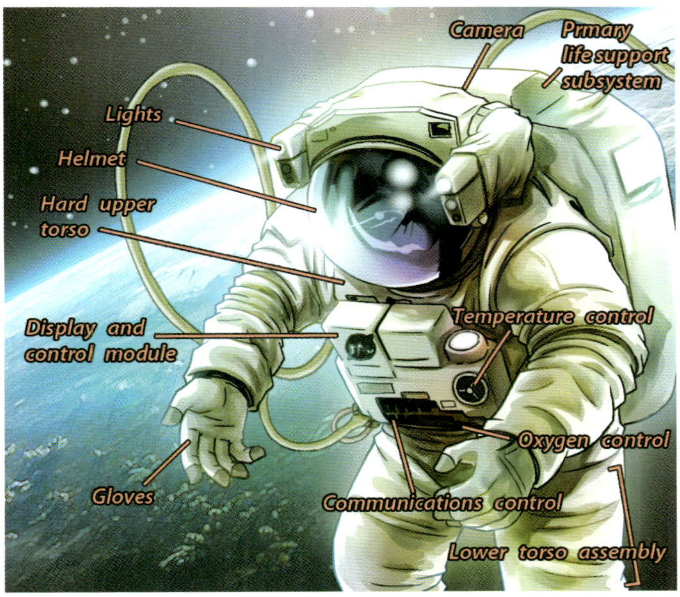

▲ Major parts of a spacesuit

On Your Own

What things do you do every day that an astronaut could not do without a spacesuit?

canister a container that can be used to hold things
communication the act of exchanging information, thoughts, or feelings
radio equipment a piece of electronic equipment that is used to communicate over a distance
ground controller someone who directs airplanes or spacecraft from a place on the ground

Vocabulary Building

[1-5] Complete each sentence with one of the words from the box.

coordinate / fluids / vacuum / insulate / exposed

1. There is a ceramic lining on the inside of the car that helps to ____________ it from heat.

2. It isn't a good idea to leave your skin ____________ too long in this hot sun.

3. If they can ____________ the exhibition with the sports events, it will be great for the city.

4. If the experiment were carried out in a(n) ____________, there would be no explosion.

5. When you are sick, it is important to drink extra ____________ to avoid dehydration.

[6-10] Choose the words that are closest in meaning to the underlined ones.

6. The proposed budget cuts will <u>eliminate</u> many jobs.

a. distribute b. promise c. require d. remove

7. The security guards <u>shield</u> the president at all times.

a. prepare b. surprise c. protect d. reward

8. The <u>fluctuation</u> of the currency has leveled off in the past year.

a. variation b. thoughtfulness c. insight d. recollection

9. She has the <u>capacity</u> to make sad people laugh.

a. ability b. formality c. experience d. truthfulness

10. People lock their doors because of the <u>potential</u> that a burglar might try to break in.

a. assurance b. possibility c. design d. fear

[11-13] Complete each sentence with the following idioms.

breathe out / deal with / build up

11. We have financial problems to ____________ before we can buy a new car.

12. If you inhale deeply and ____________ slowly, it will help you relax.

13. The company has ____________ a reputation for high-quality products over the years.

Reading Comprehension

1 What is the main idea of the passage?

a. Spacesuits make it possible for humans to survive and work in space.
b. The design of spacesuits will continue to improve as time goes on.
c. It is dangerous to work in space despite having spacesuits for protection.
d. Astronauts are able to breathe and communicate in space.

2 What function does air pressure play in supporting human life?

a. keeping the body's liquids from changing to gas
b. maintaining a livable temperature around the body
c. removing carbon dioxide after it is exhaled
d. allowing the body to move freely through the air

3 What happens when someone experiences "the bends"?

a. Nitrogen is exhaled instead of carbon dioxide.
b. The lungs cannot get enough air.
c. The body temperature rises rapidly.
d. Nitrogen bubbles appear in the blood.

4 The word sturdy in the passage is closest in meaning to

a. large b. tough
c. real d. simple

5 Which of the following is NOT provided by a spacesuit?

a. protection against small space objects
b. a supply of oxygen and nitrogen
c. the proper amount of air pressure
d. a two-way communication system

6 What can be inferred about the material out of which spacesuits are made?

a. It is smooth to the touch.
b. It can resist extreme heat.
c. It is relatively lightweight.
d. It allows oxygen to pass through.

7 What role does a spacesuit's radio system play?

8 Why does a spacesuit need to remove carbon dioxide?

9 What are micrometeoroids, and why are they dangerous?

Summary

Step 1 **Read the passage again and complete the outline with the words below.**

air pressure / radio system / astronauts / the bends / sturdy
temperature / pure oxygen / designs / guard / removed

I. The purpose of spacesuits

A. Protect ______________ outside the spacecraft

B. Provide the correct amount of ______________

II. The air inside a suit

A. Made up of ______________ to prevent "______________"

B. Dangerous carbon dioxide is ______________

III. A suit's shielding and temperature control

A. Has a(n) ______________ outer layer to ______________ against micrometeoroids

B. ______________ is kept constant

IV. Communication in space

A. Made possible by a suit's ______________

V. The evolution of spacesuits

A. ______________ of suits have changed in the past and will continue to do so

Step 2 **Complete the summary with your own words based on the outline.**

Spacesuits are designed to protect ______________ outside their spacecraft. ______________

____

____

____

____

____

____

_______ Spacesuit ______________ have changed in the past and will continue to do so.

Unit 15: Inventive Entrepreneurs

Getting Started

1. Who is the most successful businessperson you know of? How do you think that person succeeded?
2. What do you think is needed to start a business?
3. What are some inventions you can see or use in your daily life?

Building Background Knowledge

Patent

When inventors create a new device, or even when they just have an idea for one, they will usually apply for a patent. This is a set of basic rights granted to them by the government, certifying that the invention belongs to them and prohibiting others from copying it without permission. Patents only last for a certain number of years, and after this time others are no longer restricted from using the invention. Thousands of new ideas, instruments, tools, devices, and processes are patented each year. But before a patent will be issued, the Patent Office must determine that the invention is both unique and useful. For this reason, it can sometimes take a long time to receive one.

The United States of America

The Commissioner of Patents and Trademarks

Has received an application for a patent for a new and useful invention. The title and description of the invention are enclosed. The requirements of law have been complied with, and it has been determined that a patent on the invention shall be granted under the law.

Therefore, this 5,860,492

United States Patent

Grants to the person(s) having title to this patent the right to exclude others from making, using, offering for sale, or selling the invention throughout the United States of America or importing the invention into the United States of America for the term set forth below, subject to the payment of maintenance fees as provided by law.

If this application was filed prior to June 8, 1995, the term of this patent is the longer of seventeen years from the date of grant of this patent or twenty years from the earliest effective U.S. filing date of the application, subject to any statutory extension.

If this application was filed on or after June 8, 1995, the term of this patent is twenty years from the U.S. filing date, subject to any statutory extension. If the application contains a specific reference to an earlier filed application or applications under 35 U.S.C. 120, 121 or 365(c), the term of the patent is twenty years from the date on which the earliest application was filed, subject to any statutory extension.

Acting Commissioner of Patents and Trademarks

Attest

▲ Patent issued by the United States of America's Patent and Trademark Office

UNIT 15

Inventive Entrepreneurs

The Big Question

How does an invention fill an opportunity niche?

► Notes

People who start and run their own businesses are called entrepreneurs. To do this, entrepreneurs require money, or **capital**. Some can afford to **fund** their own **ventures**, but others seek loans from banks or investors. Another factor essential to building a new business is an opportunity **niche**, a need people have that is not being met by any other business. An entrepreneur attempts to fill the niche by creating a product or service.

Many of today's commonplace products were invented to fill an opportunity niche. This is what high school freshman Cody Fox did. He and his friends were tired of paying hundreds of dollars in fines for their damaged textbooks at the end of the school year. Combining an ordinary cloth book cover with a hard plastic shell, Cody invented a **practical** solution called the Book Jax. It protects textbooks from day-to-day wear, helping students return them in the same condition in which they were received. Cody's invention received a patent, and today, school supply stores around America sell the Book Jax.

▲ Book Jax

Another example is that of Humphrey O'Sullivan, who worked in a U.S. print shop in the late 1800s. His job required that he stand all day, so to minimize the strain on his feet he brought a rubber mat to the shop to stand on. The mat was so effective that O'Sullivan decided to attach rubber directly to the bottoms of his shoes. His invention was an instant

capital money or property, especially used to produce more wealth or start a business

fund to provide money for an event, activity, or organization

venture a new business project that involves financial risk

niche a specialized area of demand for a product or a service

hit, and in 1899 he patented it and started his own company to manufacture and sell his rubber-soled shoes.

▲ Sports shoes with rubber soles

► Notes

Neither Fox's nor O'Sullivan's invention was **technically** complicated or **financially** demanding. Like other successful entrepreneurs, they were simply able to identify a need and fulfill it. This demands a certain level of creativity, but another characteristic that unifies all entrepreneurs, whether or not they are inventors, is **risk** taking. They realize their ventures might fail and they could lose money. However, it can be difficult for a true entrepreneur to ignore an opportunity once he or she has spotted it. Additionally, the potential benefits of being one's own boss—the ability to make important decisions and directly reap the profits of one's labor—are too appealing for many to pass up.

On Your Own

Have you ever had an idea for an invention? What was it?

practical relating to that which is useful and can be put into effect
technically concerning special skills
financially having to do with money
risk an action attempted that carries with it the chance of failure

Vocabulary Building

[1-5] Complete each sentence with one of the words from the box.

combine / ignore / directly / complicated / strain

1. The issue is very ____________, so it will take a long time to resolve the matter.

2. Staring at the computer all day long puts a(n) ____________ on the eyes.

3. If we ____________ our two birthday parties, our friends will get to know each other.

4. I have tried to ____________ the pain, but it continues to get worse.

5. The factory sells its products ____________ to customers through the Internet.

[6-10] Choose the words that are closest in meaning to the underlined ones.

6. It's easy to find cycle paths here, because bikes are <u>commonplace</u>.

a. ordinary　　b. necessary　　c. messy　　d. knowledgeable

7. It is hard to <u>spot</u> a child in a large, moving crowd of tall adults.

a. hide　　b. call　　c. overlook　　d. find

8. Proper nutrition and exercise are <u>essential</u> to good health.

a. glamorous　　b. necessary　　c. detailed　　d. steady

9. The factory <u>manufactures</u> bicycles out of aluminum beverage cans.

a. makes　　b. locates　　c. complicates　　d. monitors

10. The president will <u>unify</u> several regions to gain power.

a. satisfy　　b. present　　c. exclude　　d. unite

[11-13] Complete each sentence with the following idioms.

make a decision / pass up / be tired of

11. We ________________ having to travel such a long way to work.

12. She didn't want to ________________ the chance to meet him, but she had to be with her family.

13. You need to ________________ about which company you want to work for by Friday.

Reading Comprehension

1 What is the main idea of the passage?

a. Inventions represent a way in which entrepreneurs can start a business.
b. Entrepreneurs typically have different characteristics than inventors.
c. It is simple to start a profitable business by marketing an invention.
d. The most significant entrepreneurial trait is that of risk taking.

2 What are two requirements for starting a business?

a. personal savings and investors who want a share of the profits
b. capital and the ability to meet a currently unfulfilled need
c. a bank loan and a commonplace product
d. investors and an entirely new invention

3 What was Cody Fox's opportunity niche?

a. friends with unpaid textbook fines
b. schools with a shortage of book covers
c. students with damaged textbooks
d. book publishers with damaged products

4 The word reap in the passage is closest in meaning to

a. collect
b. invest
c. add
d. manage

5 Which of the following is NOT mentioned as an advantage of being an entrepreneur?

a. having more control over decision-making processes
b. being able to keep profits for oneself
c. not having a boss to answer to
d. making more money than the typical employee

6 What can be inferred about Humphrey O'Sullivan?

a. His patent was later revoked.
b. He got the idea for his shoes from a coworker.
c. He suffered from a physical disability.
d. He was able to leave his job at the print shop.

7 How can people get the funds to start their own business?

8 What is the purpose of Cody Fox's Book Jax?

9 What is one characteristic that is shared by all entrepreneurs?

Summary

Step 1 **Read the passage again and complete the outline with the words below.**

capital / need / run / patent / textbook / risks
at work / creativity / niche / benefits / company / rubber

I. Entrepreneurs

A. Build and ____________ their own businesses

B. Require ____________ and an opportunity ____________ to do so

II. Cody Fox and the Book Jax

A. Saw a(n) ____________ for a protective ____________ cover

B. Invented the Book Jax and received a(n) ____________ for it

III. Humphrey O'Sullivan and rubber-soled shoes

A. Attached ____________ to his shoes to stand more comfortably ____________

B. Patented his shoes and started a(n) ____________ to sell them

IV. Traits of entrepreneurs

A. ____________ to see and respond to an opportunity niche

B. Do not mind taking ____________ in order to receive potential ____________

Step 2 **Complete the summary with your own words based on the outline.**

Entrepreneurs are people who build and ________ their own businesses. ________

____

____

____

____

____

____

Additionally, entrepreneurs take ________ in order to receive potential ________.

Unit 16: The Renaissance

Getting Started

1. Look at the picture. Do you know who drew it? What do you think the drawing tries to show?
2. What artists or scientists from the past are you most familiar with? What are they known for?
3. What do you think the most important values are in your family, at your school, and in society?

Building Background Knowledge

Between the Ancient and Modern

For Western historians, the period known as ancient history ended with the fall of the Roman Empire in 476 A.D. The next one thousand years are referred to as the Middle Ages, or Medieval period. This time is often called the Dark Ages, because the great intellectual civilizations of Greece and Rome had fallen. Life in Europe during the Middle Ages was very hard. Since most people were illiterate, the majority of power and wealth was controlled by a privileged few. Ordinary people took comfort in their Christian belief that life in heaven would relieve their suffering. Then, in the early 1400s, Europe began to experience great change. Historians call the next period of European history "the Renaissance," marking the beginning of modern history.

▲ Mona Lisa

▲ Mosaic of Jesus Christ in church of Hagia Sofia, Istanbul, Turkey

UNIT 16

The Renaissance

The Big Question

How did the Renaissance change Italy and the rest of Europe?

Notes

After the fall of Rome, Europe went through a long and difficult period known as the Dark Ages. War, poverty, and hunger spread across the continent, but by the early 1400s, parts of Europe had begun to recover. People wanted to enjoy life, and they became more interested in the world around them. This curiosity led to **creativity** in science, art, language, and learning. It was the beginning of what historians call the Renaissance—a word meaning "rebirth"—and Italy is where it started. Italy's **geographical** location made it an important trading stop during the period, and money from trade and contact with other cultures helped Italy recover from the Dark Ages before other parts of Europe.

As Italy became a center of art and learning, its people began to rediscover the values of ancient Greek and Roman artists and **thinkers**. This changed the way people viewed themselves and the world. The people of Italy moved away from the religious **philosophies** of the Middle Ages and developed a new way of thinking known as "**humanism**." Humanism emphasized the importance of individuals and taught that life could be rich and satisfying.

The powerful values of humanism transformed Italian culture. Writers started to use modern languages instead of just Latin and Greek, which the average person could not understand. Consequently, more people could read literature and learn new things. Renaissance writers wrote about daily life and encouraged people to improve themselves, be creative, and experience life to the fullest.

creativity the ability to think of or create something new
geographical having to do with geography
thinker a person who thinks carefully about important subjects or produces new ideas
philosophy a particular set of ideas and principles about life

► Notes

Similarly, Renaissance artists created more realistic images of individuals and everyday scenes. The Florentine artist Leonardo da Vinci painted his famous *Mona Lisa* and *The Last Supper*, works known for their **realism** and emotional expression. Scientists came up with new ideas as well. For example, the Italian **astronomer** Galileo Galilei made improvements in telescope technology, discovered four moons of Jupiter, and helped create the **scientific method** of investigation.

Due to the Renaissance, economic conditions and living standards in Italy rose. Other Europeans visited Italy and, impressed, started to imitate its culture and way of life. In this way, the Renaissance slowly spread north to the rest of Europe, eventually reaching France, Germany, and Poland. England was the last place in Europe to experience it. By the time of the English Renaissance in the 17th century, the continent of Europe had been thoroughly changed.

▲ Renaissance map of Europe

On Your Own

Think of one way in which your life would be different if you were living in a time before the Renaissance.

humanism a belief system that sets people at the center and views that people's needs can be satisfied without religious beliefs

realism artistic representation of things as they really are

astronomer a scientist who observes objects in space and how they move

scientific method the process through which scientists collect data to construct an accurate representation of the world

Vocabulary Building

[1-5] Complete each sentence with one of the words from the box.

continents / curiosity / emphasize / encourage / realistic

1. List the ______________ in descending order of size.

2. It is important for teachers to ______________ young learners' efforts.

3. The ______________ details on the mural are not typical of the artist's style.

4. His ______________ is part of what makes him a good student.

5. Make sure to ______________ your leadership qualities on your application form.

[6-10] Choose the words that are closest in meaning to the underlined ones.

6. I was out of school for a while and consequently fell behind in my school work.

a. therefore b. properly c. bravely d. worriedly

7. Many film directors try to imitate her style, but none are successful.

a. collect b. correct c. connect d. copy

8. The average dinner at a restaurant in New York is quite expensive.

a. horrible b. vast c. complicated d. ordinary

9. We searched the markets thoroughly to find old furniture in that style.

a. completely b. cheaply c. modestly d. helpfully

10. North Korea is a recluse nation where citizens have little contact with the outside world.

a. control b. association c. distance d. appreciation

[11-13] Complete each sentence with the following idioms.

go through / as well / due to

11. After I failed my exams, I ________________ a terrible time.

12. The café has raised its prices ________________ the failure of the coffee bean crop last year.

13. The acting class teaches students to sing and dance ________________ as act.

Reading Comprehension

1 What is the passage mainly about?

a. the causes and effects of Europe's Dark Ages
b. the influence of ancient Greece and Rome on modern Europe
c. how the Renaissance affected the arts
d. a period of important cultural changes in Europe

2 What caused the curiosity among Europeans that led to the Renaissance?

a. Soldiers who had fought in wars told stories of strange, foreign lands.
b. Religious authorities began introducing new ideas about the world.
c. Increased international trade exposed people to different cultures.
d. People had survived a difficult period and were ready to enjoy life.

3 Which was the last European country to experience the Renaissance?

a. England b. Poland
c. Germany d. France

4 The word investigation in the passage is closest in meaning to

a. search b. effect
c. formula d. medicine

5 Which of the following does NOT describe Italian art during the Renaissance?

a. It included scenes from everyday life.
b. It portrayed human forms realistically.
c. It featured images of individuals.
d. It focused on religious themes.

6 What can be inferred about the term Renaissance?

a. It applies only to the cultural changes in Italy.
b. It refers to the rebirth of old Greek and Roman ideas.
c. It was first used by Italian artists during the period.
d. It describes the rebirth of the philosophy of humanism.

7 What were the main values of humanism?

8 Why did Italy become a center of art and learning?

9 Why did Italian authors write in languages other than Greek and Latin during the Renaissance?

Summary

Step 1 **Read the passage again and complete the outline with the words below.**

individual / realistic / Leonardo da Vinci / Galileo Galilei / religion / north
curiosity / Dark Ages / England / literature / rediscovered / Italy

I. The Renaissance in Europe

A. Began around 1400, sparked by new ____________ after the ____________

B. Started in ____________, supported by money and contact from trade

II. Humanism: a new way of seeing the world

A. Influenced by ____________ ideas from ancient Greece and Rome

B. Focused on the ____________ rather than ____________

III. Results of the Italian Renaissance

A. Languages other than Greek and Latin were used in ____________

B. Artists like ____________ created more ____________ works

C. Scientists like ____________ made important discoveries and contributions

IV. Spread of the Renaissance

A. Traveled ____________ through Europe until finally reaching ____________

Step 2 **Complete the summary with your own words based on the outline.**

Europe's Renaissance began around 1400, as people developed a new __________ for life after the ____________. ____

____

____

____

____

____

______________________. __________ was the last to experience the Renaissance.

Unit 17: Time Zones

Getting Started

1 Look at the picture. Why is only half the Earth experiencing daylight?

2 Do you know why a day is 24 hours long?

3 Why do we adjust our watches when we travel?

Building Background Knowledge

Sundials

Humans first learned to measure time using shadows. They noticed that shadows were longer in the morning and grew shorter until the sun was overhead in the middle of the day. They also noticed that shadows grew longer again until evening came, and that shadows changed direction as the day passed. From such observations, they realized they could use simple sundials to tell how much of the day had passed. The first sundials probably consisted of a stick in the ground with marks drawn in the dirt around it to show the movement of the sun every hour. In ancient Egypt, tall stone towers called obelisks were built, and people told time by watching their shadows.

▲ Sundial

▲ Obelisk

UNIT 17

The Big Question

Why were time zones created?

Time Zones

18

▸ Notes

Our planet **revolves** around the sun, with one half exposed to sunlight and the other in darkness. Consequently, the half of Earth facing the sun experiences day at the same time the other half experiences night. In addition, Earth **rotates** on an imaginary line through its center called its axis. Due to Earth's rotation, different parts of the planet are constantly coming into sunlight or entering darkness.

Before clocks, people used the position of the sun to keep track of time. Its highest point in the sky represented midday. When clocks were invented, they were set according to this movement of the sun; that is, they were based on **solar time**. From town to town, clocks were set differently, according to local solar time. These differences did not matter much until the invention of railroads. Trains made it possible to travel long distances very quickly, so differences in local solar time made scheduling very confusing. Suddenly, there was a need to set a standard time.

This was done by establishing time zones. In 1884, the city of Greenwich, England, was chosen to be the world's **reference point** for keeping time, and standard time was named Greenwich Mean Time (GMT). In 1972, improvements in timekeeping technology led to the adoption of Coordinated Universal Time (UTC). UTC maintains

▲ Greenwich clock

revolve to move around something along a circular path

rotate to turn around an axis while remaining in place

solar time time measured according to the sun's movement

reference point a point to which other points or lines are referred, usually in terms of distance and direction

better accuracy than GMT by adding a **leap second** to the year whenever necessary, while still using Greenwich as a reference point.

The **physical boundaries** of the time zones were created by evenly dividing the globe into 24 sections to match the day's 24 hours. The zones were based on lines of **longitude**, the vertical lines on a map running between the north and south **poles**. Since there are 360 degrees of longitude on Earth, each time zone contains 15 degrees.

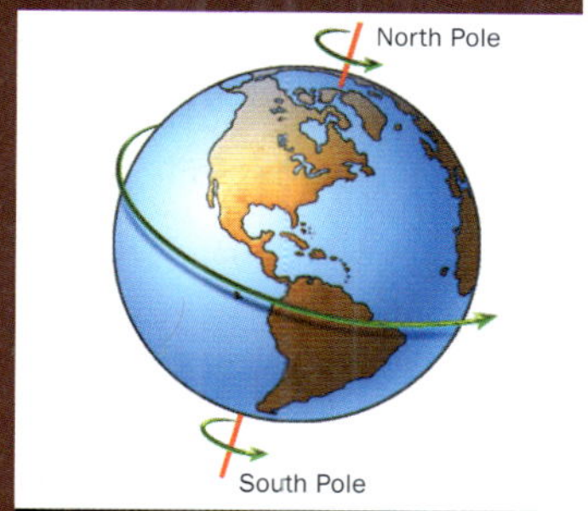

▲ Earth's rotation

Every time zone describes its local time in relation to UTC. For example, Toronto lies in the time zone that is five hours behind UTC, so the time in Toronto is written as UTC–5. At 9:22 p.m. in Greenwich, it is 4:22 p.m. in Toronto. Between time zones, only the hour changes; the minutes and seconds stay the same. When you travel east and pass into another zone, you set your watch forward one hour, while westward travel requires that you set it back one hour.

► Notes

On Your Own

When you get up for school, what do you think children on the other side of the world are doing?

leap second a positive or negative second adjusted to UTC that makes it close to astronomical time
physical boundary a mark that shows where one area ends and another starts
longitude the distance east or west of an imaginary line along the Earth's surface running North to South
pole the northernmost or southernmost point on the Earth

Vocabulary Building

[1-5] Complete each sentence with one of the words from the box.

matter / adoption / confusing / forward / vertical

1. This painting has ______________ symmetry.

2. We moved our watches ______________ three hours.

3. The ______________ of these laws will make it harder to falsely report income.

4. It is often ______________ to read legal writing, so you should ask a lawyer for help.

5. It does not ______________ how much money you have as long as you're happy.

[6-10] Choose the words that are closest in meaning to the underlined ones.

6. It would be a great thing to establish an affordable healthcare system for all citizens.

a. create b. require c. investigate d. locate

7. He maintains his garden without the use of pesticides.

a. keeps up b. affords c. corrects d. inspects

8. The vote was evenly split between the current prime minister and the opposition leader.

a. steadily b. equally c. pleasantly d. heavily

9. The chest was locked and we were highly curious about the treasures it might contain.

a. expel b. hold c. climb d. restrain

10. Sally made a slideshow of the pictures she took during her travels around the globe.

a. map b. cycle c. earth d. continent

[11-13] Complete each sentence with the following idioms.

keep track of / in relation to / lead to

11. The research focuses on mental health ___________________ life stress.

12. The nation's growing debt could ___________________ a financial crisis.

13. To ___________________ distribution, we are starting a new database.

Reading Comprehension

1 What is the passage mainly about?

a. differences between standard and local time
b. why time zones were invented
c. methods for tracking Earth's rotation
d. the role of railroads in creating time zones

2 How did people tell time traditionally?

a. by noting the movement of the sun where they lived
b. by communicating with people from nearby towns
c. by setting all the world's clocks to the same time
d. by dividing the globe into 24 time zones

3 What is true of a town in the time zone UTC–6?

a. It is six hours ahead of Greenwich.
b. It is separated from Greenwich by six degrees.
c. It is six hours behind Greenwich.
d. It is six hours from Greenwich by air.

4 The word constantly in the passage is closest in meaning to

a. almost b. usually
c. slowly d. always

5 Which of the following is NOT true about UTC?

a. The clocks of most countries are set to it.
b. It represents an improvement to GMT.
c. It uses Greenwich, England, as a reference point.
d. All time zones are measured in relation to it.

6 What can be inferred about leap seconds?

a. They are only applied to certain time zones.
b. They are not required every year.
c. They were first recommended in 1884.
d. They are added every fourth year.

7 What effect does Earth's revolution have on people around the world?

8 How did railroads encourage the creation of time zones?

9 How was it decided that each time zone would contain 15 longitudinal degrees?

Summary

Step 1 **Read the passage again and complete the outline with the words below.**

different / degrees / railroad / solar time / continually / leap
standard / zones / Greenwich / longitude / equals / half

I. Earth's revolution and rotation

A. One ______________ of Earth is in light while the other is in darkness

B. ______________ parts of Earth are ______________ entering sunlight or darkness

II. Traditional timekeeping

A. Based on each location's local ______________

B. Travel by ______________ created a need for a(n) ______________ system

III. A point of reference for time zones

A. ______________, England was chosen, creating GMT

B. UTC improved on GMT with ______________ seconds

IV. Characteristics of time zones

A. 24 ______________, each with 15 ______________, based on lines of ______________

B. One zone change ______________ one hour change, described in relation to UTC

Step 2 **Complete the summary with your own words based on the outline.**

As Earth revolves around the sun, the ____________ exposed to sunlight experiences day, while the other experiences night. ____

____

____

____

____

____

_____ One zone change ____________ one hour change, described in relation to UTC.

Unit 18: The Forces of Flight

Getting Started

1. Look at the picture. What do you think enables birds to fly?
2. Have you ever flown on an airplane? What was it like?
3. You might have heard the word "gravity" before. What do you think it means?

Building Background Knowledge

The Wright Brothers

On December 17th, 1903, the Wright brothers made history by carrying out the world's first flight in a power-driven plane. The Wright brothers were Orville and Wilbur Wright, two young bicycle mechanics who had been fascinated with machines since their childhood. After several experiments with unpowered gliders, the brothers came up with the idea of using propellers and an engine to power a small wooden plane. With Orville in the cockpit, their plane flew 36 meters in twelve seconds. The key to the Wright brother's success was an extremely precise method of testing and engineering. For example, when their test flights did not produce enough lift, they would carry out detailed scientific experiments with their homebuilt wind tunnel and balance equipment.

▲ Wright flyer

▲ A stamp showing Orville and Wilbur Wright

UNIT 18

The Forces of Flight

The Big Question

Which four forces are involved in the flight of airplanes?

► Notes

Observing birds in nature was what first inspired humans to build flying machines. The key lay in determining how wings function in lifting and **propelling** birds during flight. Although it took centuries of trial and error, **aviation** experts succeeded in designing a viable airplane. Their work was based on an understanding of the four basic forces involved in flight: lift, drag, thrust, and gravity.

Lift is the force that pulls up on an airplane and holds it in the air. The particular shape of the airplane wing produces lift, for air flows more quickly over its **curved** upper surface than it does over the flat lower surface. The faster flowing air creates a pocket of low pressure above the wing. The pressure pushing up on the wing from beneath now exceeds the pressure pushing down on the wing. Therefore, the wing rises, lifting the plane with it.

▲ Airplane propeller

The force of drag is what pushes against an object and slows it down. It is created by the air **resistance** the plane meets as it moves forward. In order to cut down on drag, airplane bodies are long and slender in form. This **streamlined** shape allows air to flow efficiently over a plane's body, minimizing the resistance it meets.

Thrust is the force that moves an airplane forward through the air,

propel to cause to move forward
aviation the science of making planes fly
curved not straight; possessing curves
resistance a force which makes a moving object slow down

and airplanes rely on a power source to generate this forward motion. In conventional planes, both engines and propellers are employed to achieve sufficient thrust for flight.

Of the four basic forces in flight, the downward force of gravity is probably the most familiar. When you stand on a bathroom **scale**, you are measuring this force's effect on your body—your weight is created by the gravitational pull of the earth. Overcoming gravity is a critical factor in flight and is another responsibility of the plane's engines.

During **stable** flight, all of the forces must be maintained in delicate balance. The **opposing forces** of lift and gravity are equal, as are the opposing forces of thrust and drag. Of course, for takeoff, the amount of lift generated must exceed the downward force of gravity acting on the plane. Likewise, in order to increase speed, a plane must apply enough thrust to overcome the force of drag.

► Notes

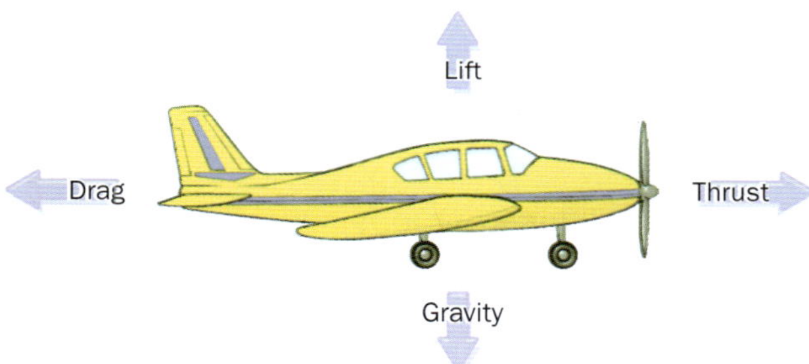

▲ Forces of flight

On Your Own

Have you ever flown in an airplane? Which of the four forces did you notice most?

streamlined designed to move efficiently and quickly through the air or water
scale an instrument that measures weight
stable not likely to move or change
opposing force a power that counteracts some other power

Vocabulary Building

[1-5] Complete each sentence with one of the words from the box.

exceed / likewise / inspire / overcome / delicate

1. He is going to buy a gift for them and I will do ____________.
2. The amount of the interest charged should not ____________ the original loan.
3. We were put in a(n) ____________ situation when asked to choose between two equally important items.
4. If you would visit museums more often, it might ____________ you to paint more.
5. It was not easy to ____________ the limitations of my illness, but I accomplished my goals.

[6-10] Choose the words that are closest in meaning to the underlined ones.

6. A <u>conventional</u> recipe for chocolate chip cookies has sugar, butter, and eggs.
   a. ordinary b. unique c. disgusting d. skillful
7. If we don't <u>generate</u> more sales, we will lose our jobs.
   a. distrust b. believe c. produce d. convince
8. Sports days are fun but there is lots of planning <u>involved</u>.
   a. included b. enjoyed c. incurred d. encouraged
9. Another <u>factor</u> that led to the decline of the empire was its sheer size.
   a. choice b. element c. declaration d. total
10. This recipe calls for a <u>particular</u> kind of cheese that comes from a small region in Italy.
    a. popular b. indifferent c. expensive d. special

[11-13] Complete each sentence with the following idioms.

slow down / pull up / cut down

11. If you would ____________ on drinking coffee, you would sleep better.
12. I need to take a few minutes to ____________ weeds from the flower beds.
13. We can ____________ the process of aging if we exercise and eat well.

Reading Comprehension

1 What is the passage mainly about?

a. historical problems with airplane development
b. the scientific principles involved in flight
c. how airplanes overcome the force of gravity
d. designing a better flying machine

2 What do an airplane's wings and its engines have in common?

a. They both affect all of the four forces of flight.
b. They produce pockets of low pressure.
c. They are designed with a streamlined shape.
d. They create forces that allow the plane to fly.

3 What happens to a plane that experiences greater drag than thrust?

a. Its speed increases.
b. Its speed decreases but its elevation increases.
c. Both its speed and elevation increase.
d. Its speed decreases.

4 The word critical in the passage is closest in meaning to

a. careful
b. dangerous
c. necessary
d. sudden

5 According to the passage, which of the following is NOT true of a plane's wings?

a. They are involved in the production of thrust.
b. During flight, pressure is greater below them.
c. Their top and bottom have different shapes.
d. They function similarly to a bird's wings.

6 What can be inferred about the force of lift that an airplane experiences?

a. It would be insufficient for flight without the plane's thrust.
b. It can be lessened by a decrease in the force of drag.
c. It may be so great that it damages the wings of the plane.
d. It must increase if the weight of the plane decreases.

7 Which forces are created by an airplane, and which ones must be overcome in order for a plane to fly?

8 Why are airplanes usually slender in shape?

9 What are two ways in which airplanes generate thrust?

Summary

Step 1 **Read the passage again and complete the outline with the words below.**

downward / forces / lift / propellers / takeoff / wings
balance / operate / thrust / increases / resistance / weight

I. How airplanes can fly

A. Airplanes ____________ according to the four ____________ of flight

II. The four forces of flight

A. ____________ is created by the plane's ____________ and pulls the plane upward

B. Drag comes from air ____________ and slows the plane down

C. ____________ is produced by the plane's engines and ____________ and moves it forward

D. Gravity acting on the ____________ of the plane pulls it ____________

III. The forces at work

A. In stable flight, the forces are kept in ____________

B. ____________ requires more lift than gravity, and speed ____________ require more thrust than drag

Step 2 **Complete the summary with your own words based on the outline.**

To understand how airplanes can fly, it is necessary to explain four scientific ________.
____
____
____
____
____
____ But during __________,
lift must outweigh gravity, and to __________ speed, thrust must outweigh drag.

Unit 19: Charles Darwin and Evolution

Getting Started

1. Look at the picture. What does it show?
2. What is the strangest insect or animal you have ever seen? What was it like?
3. When do you think the first human beings appeared on the planet?

Building Background Knowledge

Charles Darwin's School Years

As a child, Charles Darwin loved nature but hated school. Charles' father thought he was lazy, so he sent him to Edinburgh University to study medicine. Charles hated medicine and found surgery very upsetting. He much preferred to wander the Scottish coastline studying shells. Charles quit medical school and his father suggested he become a priest instead. So, Charles went to Cambridge University to study to become a priest—but he didn't enjoy that either. He spent his time collecting thousands of beetles and putting them in boxes. Fortunately, at Cambridge he met Professor Henslow, a plant expert, and Professor Sedgwick, a rock specialist. They encouraged Charles and taught him how to study nature scientifically. Finally Charles Darwin had found a subject he loved!

▲ Cambridge University

UNIT 19

Charles Darwin and Evolution

The Big Question

What was Darwin's primary contribution to science?

► Notes

The British scientist Charles Darwin introduced the modern theory of **evolution**, forever altering our ideas about life on Earth. Born into a wealthy English family in 1809, Darwin showed a fascination with nature from an early age, collecting rocks, plants, and animals that he found. His father sent him to Edinburgh to study medicine, and then to Cambridge to become a priest, but neither profession interested Darwin. At Cambridge, he was tutored in science by the **botanist** J. S. Henslow. Henslow also introduced Darwin to ship captain Robert FitzRoy, who, in 1831, invited Darwin to accompany him on a mapmaking expedition to South America. He accepted, not realizing the journey would change his life.

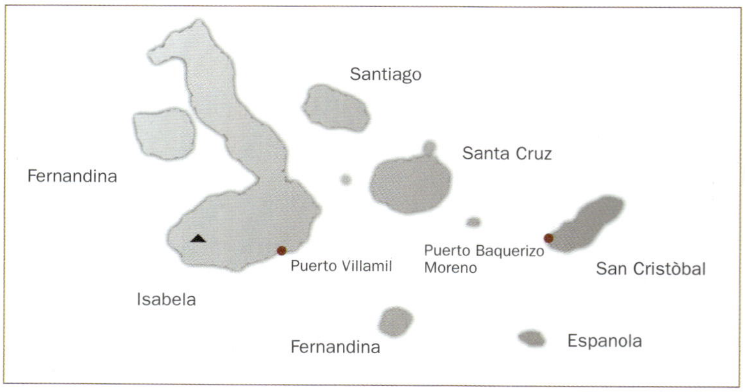

▲ Galapagos Islands

The trip lasted five years, during which Darwin read a book called *Principles of* ***Geology***. Its author claimed that Earth was millions of years old and was continuously changing. This was a revolutionary notion at the time, but Darwin's observations seemed to support it. Moreover, he started thinking the same was true of life on Earth. On South America's isolated Galapagos Islands, he encountered several **finch** populations. The finches' characteristics

evolution the process in which animals and plants change and develop gradually over a long period of time

botanist a scientist that studies plants

geology a branch of science concerned with the history of the Earth and its physical features

finch a kind of small songbird that has a cone-shaped bill

were closely related but varied from island to island in important ways. Darwin collected many animal **specimens**, including these finches, for further study in England.

Back home, he showed the birds to an expert, who reported that Darwin had gathered finches from 13 different species, not just one. For the next 20 years, Darwin attempted to develop an explanation for how species like those of the 13 finches had evolved. His answer was a theory of evolution by **natural selection**. The theory is based on the idea that the individuals of a species are all slightly different, and some differences help one individual survive better than another. The survivors have more opportunities to **reproduce**, and genetic traits are passed from parent to child. Gradually, specific traits come to **dominate** a population, and over generations different populations can transform into new species. In 1859, Darwin published his theory in a book titled *On the Origin of Species*.

At first, most people rejected Darwin's ideas. They believed God had created the world just as it was and found the notion of evolution unacceptable. There remains some religious objection to Darwin's theory among the general public even today. However, the theory has the proof of science behind it and has become one of the central principles of biology.

▸ Notes

▲ Charles Darwin

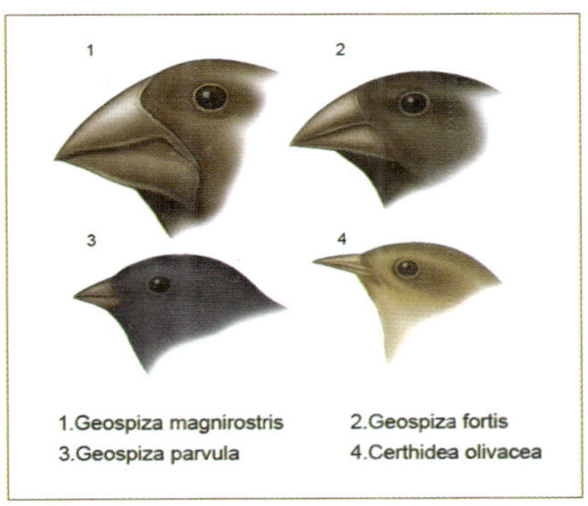

▲ Finches from Galapagos Islands

On Your Own

When you were younger, did you ever collect objects you found in nature?

specimen a sample of something that is to be studied scientifically
natural selection the process through which genes are passed on or eliminated
reproduce to bear offspring
dominate to strongly influence

Vocabulary Building

[1-5] Complete each sentence with one of the words from the box.

fascination / expedition / trait / encountered / reject

1. When I was camping last summer I _____________ a bear.

2. The researcher went on a dangerous _____________ to map remote areas.

3. It is a human _____________ to try to define and classify the things we find in the world.

4. You shouldn't simply _____________ an idea just because it is different from your own.

5. You must have a deep _____________ with the subject to have devoted so much of your time to it.

[6-10] Choose the words that are closest in meaning to the underlined ones.

6. In these myths, we see that attempts to <u>alter</u> fate are never successful.

a. release b. abuse c. recommend d. change

7. The <u>notion</u> of traveling by sailboat to Japan is not a bad one.

a. idea b. attempt c. pretend d. justice

8. Being a lawyer is a good <u>profession</u> for people who write well.

a. framework b. pastime c. occupation d. victory

9. To be eligible for the offer, you must provide <u>proof</u> of income.

a. evidence b. support c. fiction d. loyalty

10. The store only accepts one <u>specific</u> type of credit card.

a. close b. careful c. vague d. particular

[11-13] Complete each sentence with the following idioms.

millions of / over generations / for further study

11. _________________ insects are eaten by spiders every year.

12. At the end of each chapter, you will find suggestions _________________.

13. _________________, the tribe learned to survive in the harsh desert climate.

Reading Comprehension

1 What is the main idea of the passage?

a. Darwin's theory is one among several different possible explanations of evolution.
b. Darwin's sea voyage prompted him to develop a groundbreaking theory of evolution.
c. Darwin drew on ideas from Henslow and FitzRoy to create his famous theory.
d. Darwin was deeply affected by the public opposition to his work.

2 What concept in *Principles of Geology* inspired Darwin on his voyage?

a. Life on Earth began millions of years in the past.
b. The planet is millions of years old and always changing.
c. All forms of life descended from a common ancestor.
d. Isolated islands have unique life forms living on them.

3 What was the purpose of FitzRoy's journey to South America?

a. to create maps
b. to study geology
c. to collect animal specimens
d. to research a theory of evolution

4 The word accompany in the passage is closest in meaning to

a. go with b. talk to c. guide d. take care of

5 Which of the following is NOT part of Darwin's theory?

a. Every member within a species is slightly different.
b. Some individuals' traits are more advantageous than others.
c. Species living in isolated environments evolve faster than others.
d. Individuals with the best survival traits come to dominate the population.

6 What can be inferred about the field of geology in the time of Darwin?

a. It stated that Earth was constantly changing.
b. It was in its earliest stages of development.
c. It did not explain the formation of islands.
d. It taught that Earth was relatively young.

7 According to Darwin's theory, how do species evolve?

8 Which professions did Darwin reject before finding his calling as an explorer and scientist?

9 Why have some people always objected to the theory of evolution?

Summary

Step 1 **Read the passage again and complete the outline with the words below.**

careers / finches / nature / specimens / controversial / evolve
collected / biology / theory / accompanied / natural selection / published

I. Darwin's early life

A. Was fascinated with ______________ and ______________ objects

B. Was not interested in the ______________ his father directed him toward

II. Darwin's voyage

A. ______________ FitzRoy to South America and read *Principles of Geology*

B. Collected animal ______________, including Galapagos ______________

III. After the voyage

A. Worked on a(n) ______________ to explain his observations

B. Theorized that a species could ______________ over time

C. ______________ the book, *On the Origin of Species*

IV. The effect of Darwin's book

A. ______________ ideas about God and evolution

B. Theory of evolution by ______________ became central principle of ______________

Step 2 **Complete the summary with your own words based on the outline.**

Early in life, Darwin showed an interest in __________ rather than in the __________ his father directed him towards. ____

____

____

____

____

____ Nonetheless, Darwin's theory of evolution by ________________ became one of the central principles of __________.

Unit 20: Michelangelo and the Sistine Chapel Ceiling

The Creation of Adam, part of the fresco on the Vatican's Sistine Chapel

Getting Started

1. Look at the picture. Do you know where it is from?
2. What do you think the painting depicts? Do you recognize any of the characters?
3. Have you ever been inside a chapel? If so, what did you see there?

Building Background Knowledge

Frescoes

Frescoes are paintings which are done on plaster, a material often spread across ceilings and walls. Plaster starts as a powder that, when mixed with water, becomes a thick paste which eventually hardens. The word fresco comes from an Italian word meaning "fresh." This is because frescoes are painted directly onto fresh plaster which is still slightly wet. The artist then has about ten hours in which to finish a painting before the plaster dries. For this reason, many frescoes are done in sections rather than all at once. The artist can decide how much he or she can paint at one time and mix enough plaster for that area. Then the artist rests before starting a new section.

▲ Fresco on the facade of a notary office in Hayange, Moselle, France

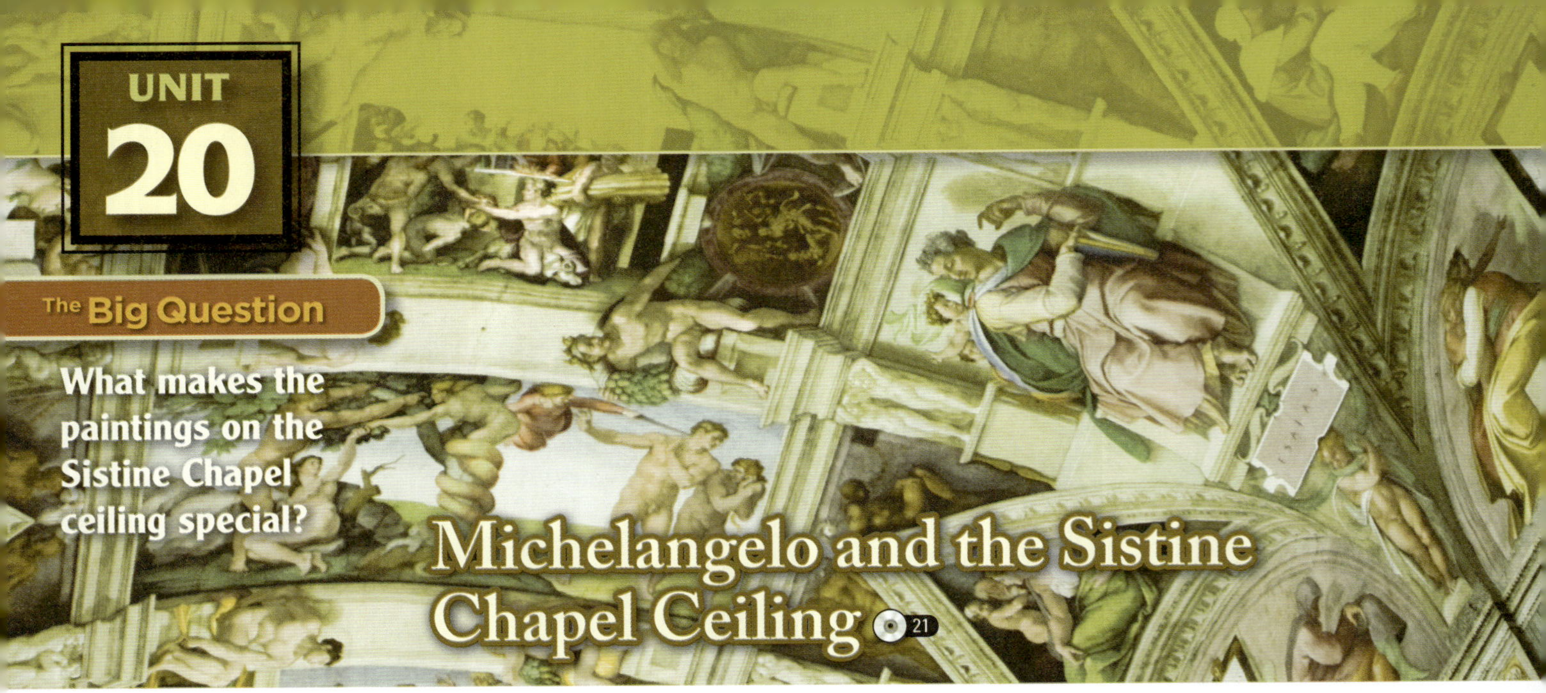

UNIT 20

The Big Question

What makes the paintings on the Sistine Chapel ceiling special?

Michelangelo and the Sistine Chapel Ceiling

▸ Notes

The Sistine **Chapel**, constructed in Vatican City between 1475 and 1483, is best known for its 12,000-square-foot ceiling, painted by the artist Michelangelo in the early 1500s. The project was commissioned by Pope Julius II. Though Michelangelo preferred **sculpture** to painting and knew the job would be quite challenging, he could not refuse the Pope.

In 1508, Michelangelo began painting frescoes on the massive ceiling. Of course, Michelangelo had to find a way to reach the 68-foot-high ceiling first. He built a wooden **platform** that attached to the chapel walls. Lying on his back on the platform, he applied fresco plaster and paint to the ceiling directly above him. It was an uncomfortable but necessary position for accessing the ceiling. Working in this fashion, it took him four years to complete the entire project.

In addition to the discomfort caused by painting upside down, Michelangelo faced other obstacles. Early in the project, he discovered that his plaster was too wet. **Mold** was growing on and inside it and causing it to crumble. In early 1509, he was forced to destroy his progress and start over, using an innovative plaster recipe that later became the standard for Italian fresco painters. Another problem was that the Pope neglected to pay Michelangelo the money he was due. Because he was spending all his time on the

▲ Michelangelo

chapel a building which is used for Christian worship
sculpture the art of making objects out of a material such as stone, wood, or clay
platform a tall, flat structure on which people can stand or work
mold a soft, green or gray substance that grows on old food or on objects that are in warm, wet air

chapel, this nearly drove the artist to poverty. When he finally finished in 1512, he was exhausted and his eyesight was suffering.

Fortunately, his creation was immediately recognized as a masterpiece. The Pope had originally requested paintings of the twelve **apostles** only, but Michelangelo greatly expanded on this. He divided the central length of the ceiling into nine **panels**, each showing a scene from the Book of **Genesis**. The image of God reaching out to give life to Adam, perhaps the most famous image of the entire work, occupies one of these panels. Surrounding the central row are **biblical figures** and scenes from other well-known Bible stories, such as David and Goliath. In addition to the great scale of the work, what most impressed onlookers was the precise detail with which the human forms had been painted. Michelangelo's mastery encouraged other painters to adopt a more realistic style and changed the direction of Western art.

▸ Notes

▲ The Statue of David, completed by Michelangelo in 1504

On Your Own

Have you ever painted a picture? What did you paint?

the apostles the group of early Christians who taught and spread the Christian religion

panel a flat and usually rectangular piece of material that forms part of a door, wall, etc.

Genesis the first book of the Bible, which describes how God created the world

biblical figure an important or famous character in or relating to the Bible

Vocabulary Building

[1-5] Complete each sentence with one of the words from the box.

access / obstacle / innovative / occupy / precise

1. His job allows him to ______________ many people in the movie business.

2. A lack of talent is more of a(n) ______________ than a lack of money.

3. They are looking for someone to ______________ their house while they are away.

4. Baking, unlike some other kinds of cooking, requires ______________ measurement.

5. That company is famous for its ______________ technological contributions.

[6-10] Choose the words that are closest in meaning to the underlined ones.

6. My sister, an interior designer, has been <u>commissioned</u> to redecorate the governor's mansion.

a. fired b. hired c. retired d. wired

7. The walls around the ancient city have begun to <u>crumble</u>.

a. debate b. grind c. enlarge d. disintegrate

8. You'll be <u>exhausted</u> if you try to drive to the country after working 10 hours.

a. fatigued b. precious c. terrified d. excited

9. Because of the mayor's <u>neglect</u>, the old bridge has become dangerous.

a. illness b. approval c. disregard d. sucess

10. The <u>onlookers</u> cheered on the basketball players from the stands.

a. participants b. spectators c. reporters d. fans

[11-13] Complete each sentence with the following idioms.

be known for / upside down / reach out

11. The paper ________________ its neutral reporting of elections.

12. She made a huge mess when she turned the full glass ________________.

13. ________________ and grab a piece of fruit from the tree if your arms are long enough.

Reading Comprehension

1 What is the main idea of the passage?

a. Michelangelo overcame many difficulties to produce an artistic masterpiece.
b. The Sistine Chapel is an impressive example of religious architecture.
c. Michelangelo painted mostly religious themes throughout his career.
d. The Pope and Michelangelo did not agree on a design for the Sistine Chapel ceiling.

2 How did Michelangelo's work influence later art?

a. It discouraged the use of frescoes.
b. It led to more paintings in religious buildings.
c. It promoted a more detailed style.
d. It made painting human forms more acceptable.

3 Why did Michelangelo have to build a wooden platform?

a. to supervise the work of other painters
b. to gain access to the tall ceiling
c. to support the weight of the fresco plaster
d. to plan out the design of his paintings

4 The word challenging in the passage is closest in meaning to

a. beautiful   b. difficult
c. famous   d. careful

5 Which of the following was NOT a problem Michelangelo faced in painting the chapel ceiling?

a. convincing the Pope to hire him
b. lying in an uncomfortable position
c. a lack of money
d. an unusable plaster recipe

6 What can be inferred about Michelangelo's other works?

a. They were paid for by the Pope.
b. They include an abundance of statues.
c. They are mostly religious in nature.
d. They are not as well known.

7 What did Michelangelo primarily paint on the ceiling of the Sistine Chapel?

8 What effect did the project have on Michelangelo physically?

9 What are two examples of scenes from the Sistine Chapel ceiling?

Summary

Step 1 **Read the passage again and complete the outline with the words below.**

pay / uncomfortable / asked for / frescoes / Bible / influenced
detail / masterpiece / create / ceiling / Pope / expansive

I. The project: painting the Sistine Chapel ____________

A. Michelangelo did not want to, but he could not say no to the ____________

B. The painting was done with ____________

II. Problems faced by Michelangelo

A. He had to lie in a(n) ____________ position in order to paint

B. He had to ____________ a new plaster recipe after his first one failed

C. The Pope did not ____________ him for his work

III. The final result: a(n) ____________

A. Was more ____________ than what the Pope originally ____________

B. Featured people and scenes from different ____________ stories

C. Showed an extraordinary amount of ____________ and ____________ other painters

Step 2 **Complete the summary with your own words based on the outline.**

Michelangelo was asked by the ________ to paint the Sistine Chapel. ____________

____

____

____

____

____

____

The extraordinary ________ Michelangelo used greatly ____________ other painters.

Supplementary Material

(Write & Speak)

Unit 1

Write and Speak

The Big Question

Some schools have strict rules and some schools don't. Which do you prefer?

A. Place a check (✔) next to the rules that are enforced at your school. For number 8, think of one more school rule and write it down.

1. We must wear school uniforms. ☐
2. We must take off our hats in class. ☐
3. We must attach name tags to our school uniforms. ☐
4. We must not run in the hallway at school. ☐
5. We are not allowed to chew gum in class. ☐
6. We are not allowed to grow our hair long. ☐
7. We are not allowed to use cell phones at school. ☐
8. We ______________________________

B. Considering your school situation, do you prefer strict rules or relaxed rules? Give two reasons for your preference.

Type of school rules	Reasons for preference
	1.
	2.

C. Using your ideas from Questions A and B, write a paragraph answering The Big Question at the top of this page. Share your answer with the class.

My school has ______________________________.

We ______________________________.

Because of this, ______________________________.

______________________________.

I would prefer that ______________________________.

Unit 2

Write and Speak

The Big Question

Climate change affects people around the world. What do you think we can do to stop it?

A. Has global climate change affected the summers and winters in your country? In the list below, place a check (✔) next to the changes you have noticed in each season. If you can think of other changes, write them down.

Summer	**Winter**
☐ rains a lot / flooding	☐ snows a lot / snowstorm
☐ rains less / drier	☐ snows less / rains more
☐ more humid	☐ drier
☐ strong sunlight	☐ warmer
☐ hotter	☐ colder
☐ longer season	☐ longer season
☐ shorter season	☐ shorter season
______________	______________

B. Think of three things you can do to stop climate change and write them down.

1. ____.
2. ____.
3. ____.

C. Using your ideas from Questions A and B, write a paragraph answering The Big Question at the top of this page. Share your answer with the class.

My country is getting __________ *because of climate change. The summers are* __________.

____

____

____

Therefore, we should ____.

Unit 3

Write and Speak

The Big Question

What would it be like if we only saw the world in black and white? What things would be affected, and what things would not seem different?

A. Place a check (✔) next to the things that would be different in a black-and-white world. In the blanks, write down anything else that would be affected.

- ☐ Fashion & hairstyles
- ☐ Reading & writing
- ☐ Food
- ☐ Black & white movies
- ☐ Traffic lights
- ______________
- ☐ Cars
- ☐ Speaking
- ☐ Color movies
- ☐ Dance/ Music
- ☐ Family
- ______________

B. Choose one thing that would be affected by a black-and-white world and write the reason why.

Affected	Why it would be affected

Choose one thing that would NOT be affected by a black-and-white world and write the reason why.

Not Affected	Why it would not be affected

C. Using your ideas from Questions A and B, write a paragraph answering The Big Question at the top of this page. Share your answer with the class.

If the world did not have any color, ______________________________.

____

____

____

______________________________.

Unit 4

Write and Speak

The Big Question

The food chain is made up of herbivores, carnivores, and omnivores. Which group do the people in your country belong to?

A. Place a check (✔) next to the foods eaten by people in your country. Write down any other food items you can think of in the blanks.

☐ chicken
☐ bacon
☐ steak
☐ milk
☐ fish
☐ rice
____

☐ bread
☐ salad
☐ pickles
☐ oranges
☐ apples
☐ peanuts
____

B. Considering the foods you checked in Question A, do you think people in your country are carnivores, herbivores, or omnivores? Give reasons for your answer.

Carnivores, herbivores, or omnivores?	Why people in your country belong to this category
	1.
	2.

C. Using your ideas from Questions A and B, write a paragraph answering The Big Question at the top of this page. Share your answer with the class.

I believe people in my country are ______________________________.

____

____

____

______________________________.

Unit 5

Write and Speak

The Big Question

Imagine that you are in charge of inventing your own style of pancake. What would it look and taste like?

A. Place a check (✔) next to the shapes and toppings you would like for your pancake. If you don't see the shapes and toppings you want, write them down and add them to the list. Then, in the space next to the list, try to draw your pancake.

Shapes	**Toppings**
☐ rabbit	☐ maple syrup
☐ cat face	☐ strawberry
☐ smiley face	☐ blueberry
☐ tortoise	☐ tomatoes
☐ thin	☐ nuts
☐ big	☐ sour cream
________	________

B. Explain your choice of shapes and toppings.

Shapes and toppings	Why you chose it
Shapes: ________ ________	
Toppings: ________ ________	

C. Using your ideas from Questions A and B, write a paragraph answering The Big Question at the top of this page. Share your answer with the class.

My pancake would look like ________________________________.

____

____

____

________________________________.

Unit 6

Write and Speak

The Big Question

Roman children studied a variety of subjects in school, such as Latin, grammar, literature, and public speaking, as well as reading, writing, and math. Among these subjects, which would you want to study? Why?

A. In the box below, look at the list of subjects that Roman children studied. Then write down why it would be important for Roman children to study them.

Subjects	Reasons for studying the subjects
Latin	
Greek	
Public speaking	
Math	
Grammar	
Reading	
Literature	
Writing	

B. Choose the subject from the list above that you would want to study the most. Explain why you want to study it.

Subject	Reasons for wanting to study it

C. Using your ideas from Questions A and B, write a paragraph answering The Big Question at the top of this page. Share your answer with the class.

I'd like to study ________________________________.

____

____

____

________________________________.

Unit 7

Write and Speak

The Big Question

Flags say many things about the values and characteristics of the people who fly them. If you had to design a flag for your family, what would it look like?

A. Place a check (✔) next to the characteristics you would want your flag to have. Write down any additional colors or shapes you can think of in the blanks. Then in the space on the right, try to draw your family flag.

Colors
- ☐ blue
- ☐ red
- ☐ pink
- ☐ purple
- ☐ green
- ☐ yellow
- ________

Shapes
- ☐ heart
- ☐ circle
- ☐ rectangle
- ☐ square
- ☐ triangle
- ☐ oval
- ________

B. Explain what each color and shape you chose represents.

Colors and shapes		What they represent
Colors		
Shapes		

C. Using your ideas from Questions A and B, write a paragraph answering The Big Question at the top of this page. Share your answer with the class.

I would make my family flag have ________________________________.

They would represent ________________________________

____

____

________________________________.

Unit 8

Write and Speak

The Big Question

It is often said that certain sounds make us feel good. What sounds do you like? Why?

A. Place a check (✔) next to the sounds you enjoy hearing. Write down any other sounds you like in the blanks.

- ☐ chime bell
- ☐ tap dancing
- ☐ stream
- ☐ woodpecker
- ☐ fireworks
- ________
- ☐ bee
- ☐ raindrop
- ☐ wind
- ☐ frog
- ☐ dog
- ________

B. Choose the sound that you like the most. Explain why you like it.

Your favorite sound	Reasons for liking the sound
	1.
	2.

C. Using your ideas from Questions A and B, write a paragraph answering The Big Question at the top of this page. Share your answer with the class.

My favorite sound is ________________________________.

____

____

____

________________________________.

Unit 9

Write and Speak

The Big Question

There are proven ways to strengthen your immune system. How would you put some of them into practice in your daily life?

A. The following are natural ways to boost your immune system. Place a check (✔) next to any that you don't practice in your life.

☐ Work out regularly.
☐ Get at least seven hours of sleep.
☐ Eat green vegetables.
☐ Eat fruits high in vitamin C such as oranges, apples, and kiwis.
☐ Try to laugh as much as you can.
☐ Avoid sweets and high-fat food items.

B. Choose two things from the list above that you would like to put into practice in your life. Then describe how you would change your habits to make them possible.

Ways to strengthen the immune system	Changes in habit to make them possible
1.	
2.	

C. Using your ideas from Questions A and B, write a paragraph answering The Big Question at the top of this page. Share your answer with the class.

I am going to strengthen my immune system by ______________________.

____

____

____

______________________.

Unit 10

Write and Speak

The Big Question

Imagine you could choose to compete in an Olympic sport. Which sport would you choose and why?

A. Place a check (✔) next to at least two sports you are good at or interested in learning.

☐ swimming
☐ soccer
☐ taekwondo
☐ gymnastics
☐ cycling
☐ wrestling
☐ boxing

☐ volleyball
☐ tennis
☐ badminton
☐ archery
☐ table tennis
☐ marathon
☐ modern pentathlon

B. If you were to compete in the Olympics and had to choose one of the sports you checked in Question A, which sport would you choose? Explain why you chose the sport.

Name of sport	Why I chose the sport
	1.
	2.

C. Using your ideas from Questions A and B, write a paragraph answering The Big Question at the top of this page. Share your answer with the class.

I would like to participate in the Olympics as a ________________. ____________________

____

____

____

____.

Unit 11

Write and Speak

The Big Question

Suppose you built a huge castle in Europe. What would you include within your castle walls? Why?

A. Place a check (✔) next to all the things you would want in your castle. Write down any other ideas you may have for your castle.

❐ banquet room
❐ tall tower
❐ moat
____

❐ chapel
❐ armory
❐ garden
____

B. Choose two things from the list above that you would most want to include in your castle. Explain why you would like to include them.

Items or rooms in your castle	Why you would want them in your castle
1.	
2.	

C. Using your ideas from Questions A and B, write a paragraph answering The Big Question at the top of this page. Share your answer with the class.

My castle would have ______________________________.

____

____

____

______________________________.

Unit 12

Write and Speak

The Big Question

Imagine you have some money to invest. How would you choose to invest it and why?

A. Below are some ways to invest money. Place a check (✔) next to the one you would use to increase your investment. Write down any other investment ideas you can think of.

☐ buying stocks
☐ putting money in a savings account
☐ buying antiques or paintings
____

B. Explain why you chose the option in Question A.

Your investment option	The reasons for your choice
	1.
	2.

C. Using your ideas from Questions A and B, write a paragraph answering The Big Question at the top of this page. Share your answer with the class.

I would ______________________________.
____
____
____
______________________________.

Unit 13

Write and Speak

The Big Question

A block of steel will sink in the water, while a heavy steel ship will float. Using the theory of buoyancy, explain the reason why a steel ship will float.

A. Place a check (✔) next to the traits of a steel ship that help it float. Write down any other traits you can think of.

☐ motor
☐ solid
☐ boat-shaped
☐ hollow and filled with air
☐ metallic
☐ human crew
☐ total weight vs. displaced water

____

B. Choose two or more traits from the list above that help a steel ship float according to the theory of buoyancy. Explain how these traits affect the ship.

Trait	How it helps the ship float

C. Using your ideas from Questions A and B, write a paragraph answering The Big Question at the top of this page. Share your answer with the class.

A steel ship is ______________________________.

____

____

____

______________________________.

Unit 14

Write and Speak

The Big Question

If you could take a space trip, what would you do? Where would you want to go? Why?

A. Place a check (✔) next to the things you would want to do during your space trip and the planets that you would want to visit. Write down any other ideas or planets you can think of.

Things to do

- ☐ Eat space food
- ☐ See the Earth from outer space
- ☐ Dance in zero gravity
- ☐ Take a spacewalk
- ☐ Put on a spacesuit
- ☐ Pilot a space shuttle
- ______________________

Planet

- ☐ Mercury
- ☐ Venus
- ☐ Mars
- ☐ Jupiter
- ☐ Saturn
- ☐ Uranus
- ☐ Neptune
- ________

B. Choose one planet you would want to visit and two things you would most want to do on your space trip. Explain why you chose them.

Planet and activities		Why you chose them
Planet		
Things to do	1.	
	2.	

C. Using your ideas from Questions A and B, write a paragraph answering The Big Question at the top of this page. Share your answer with the class.

I would choose to visit __________ *because* ________________________________.

____

____

____

____.

Unit 15

Write and Speak

The Big Question

There were a number of significant inventions during the last century. Which invention do you think has had the biggest impact on your life today?

A. Place a check (✔) next to the items and products that you and your family often use. Write down any other inventions from the last century you can think of.

☐ Internet
☐ cell phone
☐ microwave
☐ laser
☐ airplane
____

☐ digital music player
☐ Post-it
☐ car
☐ ballpoint pen
____

B. Choose the one invention that has had the biggest impact on your life. Explain why the invention is important.

Invention	Why the invention is important

C. Using your ideas from Questions A and B, write a paragraph answering The Big Question at the top of this page. Share your answer with the class.

Among the greatest inventions of the last century, I think ________________________.

____

____

____

____.

Unit 16

Write and Speak

The Big Question

During the Renaissance, writers encouraged people to live life to the fullest. What does experiencing life to the fullest mean to you?

A. Place a check (✔) next to any of the following ideas that would help you live your life to the fullest. Write down any additional ideas you may have in the blank.

☐ volunteering to help the less fortunate
☐ traveling around the world to see different places
☐ having extensive knowledge in many fields
☐ being active in protecting the environment

____

B. Choose one of the above ideas and explain why it helps you to live your life to the fullest.

Idea	Why the idea helps you to live your life to the fullest

C. Using your ideas from Questions A and B, write a paragraph answering The Big Question at the top of this page. Share your answer with the class.

I think ____.

____

____

____

____.

Unit 17

Write and Speak

The Big Question

Many countries set their clocks forward one hour in the summer ("Daylight Savings Time") so that mornings and afternoons have more daylight while evenings have less. What do you think is the most important benefit of this?

A. The following are some benefits that Daylight Savings Time could bring about. In the blanks, write down any additional benefits you can think of.

- energy savings
- safer commutes to work and school
- an increase in leisure time
- ______________________________
- ______________________________
- ______________________________

B. Choose one of the benefits of Daylight Savings Time. Explain why it is important to you and your society.

Benefit	Why it is important

C. Using your ideas from Questions A and B, write a paragraph answering The Big Question at the top of this page. Share your answer with the class.

Daylight Savings Time can ______________________________.

____

____

____

______________________________.

Unit 18

Write and Speak

The Big Question

Airplanes and helicopters are the most common forms of flight. If you were taking a trip, where would you go? If you could choose between an airplane and a helicopter, which would you use on your trip?

A. Write "A" next to the statements that describe the advantages of airplanes and "H" for those that describe the advantages of helicopters. In the blank, write down any additional characteristics of either form of flight you can think of.

____ It can take off and land anywhere.
____ It is faster and can travel longer distances.
____ It can move vertically.
____ It makes less noise during take-off and flight.
____

B. Choose a destination you would like to visit on your holiday. Then, choose either an airplane or a helicopter for your mode of travel and give two reasons for your choice.

Your destination	Why you prefer an airplane or a helicopter

C. Using your ideas from Questions A and B, write a paragraph answering The Big Question at the top of this page. Share your answer with the class.

I would choose to go to ____________ *by* ____________. *First of all,* ______________

____

____

____

____.

Unit 19

Write and Speak

The Big Question

Darwin's journey was a life-changing experience for him. What experience in your life has influenced you the most or changed the way you think?

A. Look at the pictures below and think about an important experience in your life. Then write down two ways in which the experience has changed you.

Experience	How the experience changed you
	1.
	2.

B. Using your ideas from Question A, write a paragraph answering The Big Question at the top of this page. Share your answer with the class.

The experience that has influenced me the most is ______________________.

____

____

____

____.

Unit 20

Write and Speak

The Big Question

The Sistine Chapel is one of Italy's most famous landmarks. Every country has its own famous landmarks. Which landmark do you want to visit and why?

A. Place a check (✔) next to the landmarks that you want to visit. If the landmark you wish to visit is not pictured, write the name of the landmark and its country in the blanks.

☐ The Statue of Liberty / U.S.A.
☐ The Taj Mahal / India
☐ The Eiffel Tower / France
☐ The Great Wall / China

____________ / ____________

B. From the list above, choose one landmark that you especially want to visit. Explain why you would like to visit this landmark.

Landmark	Why you want to visit the landmark
	1.
	2.

C. Using your ideas from Questions A and B, write a paragraph answering The Big Question at the top of this page. Share your answer with the class.

I'd like to visit ____________ *in* ____________. ________________________

____

____

____

____.

Unit 1

Word	Definition	Translation
empire	*n.* many lands that are ruled by one leader	
irrigation canal	*n.* a path made for water to be used for crops	
grid	*n.* a pattern of lines that are crossed in a planned way	
taxation	*n.* a requirement that people pay money to their government	
punishment	*n.* unpleasant consequences for actions that break laws or rules	
justice	*n.* maintaining fairness among people	
slab	*n.* a thick piece of material like stone or wood	
government	*n.* an organization that has political rule over a certain area or population	
conquer	*v.* to overtake by force in battle or war *syn.* defeat	
illegal	*adj.* not following the rule of law *syn.* unlawful	
inflict	*v.* to make someone experience unpleasantness *syn.* impose	
distribute	*v.* to hand something out over an area or among people *syn.* spread	
influence	*v.* to have an effect on a person or a situation *syn.* impact	
principle	*n.* a strong belief that people act on *syn.* rule	
predecessor	*n.* one who comes before another	
orderly	*adj.* in a planned and peaceful way *syn.* organized	
describe	*v.* to talk or write about the details of something *syn.* tell about	
massive	*adj.* extremely large and heavy *syn.* colossal	
put on display	to leave something out for others to see *syn.* show	
in fact	the way things are in reality *syn.* really	
such as	in the same way *syn.* for example	

Unit 2

Word	Definition	Translation
climate	*n.* the pattern of weather in an area of the world	
plain	*n.* a large area of land that is mostly flat and dry	
ecological	*adj.* related to the interaction between plants and animals and their environment	
transitional	*adj.* related to conditions that are changing	
plateau	*n.* an area of land that is mostly flat and at a higher elevation than the area surrounding it	
oasis	*n.* a place in a desert with water and trees	
vegetation	*n.* the plant life in a certain area	
tropical	*adj.* of or occurring in a moist and generally warm climate	
flat	*adj.* level having a surface that remains the same and is not curved	
survive	*v.* to continue to live	
ideal	*adj.* perfect ; exactly meeting expectations	
distance	*n.* expanse ; amount of space between people, places or things	
landscape	*n.* the combined physical features of a large area of nature	
environment	*n.* the relationship between climate, water, soil and living things	
affect	*v.* to make a change in something	
characteristic	*n.* a particular trait of some person or thing *syn.* feature	
receive	*v.* to be given something *syn.* get	
crop	*n.* fruit and vegetables that come from a seasonal harvest	
think ahead	to plan in advance	
be crowded with	having a high concentration of something	
have (little) room for	(not) possessing adequate space	

Unit 3

Word	Definition	Translation
energy	*n.* the capacity that something has to work, move or bring about change *syn.* power	
source	*n.* the beginning, or the starting point of something *syn.* origin	
wave	*n.* a line that rises and falls	
bounce off	*v.* to move away from a surface as the result of striking it	
reflection	*n.* the action of light or sound changing direction as a result of bouncing off a surface	
prism	*n.* a transparent block of glass that can divide white light into different colors	
spectrum	*n.* the range of colors in white light, visible when separated by a prism	
coal	*n.* a black, dense matter that can be burned as fuel	
object	*n.* an entity that is not living *syn.* thing	
absorb	*v.* to draw in	
separate	*v.* to move or keep things away from each other *syn.* part	
analyze	*v.* to carefully consider the parts that make up some situation *syn.* dissect	
direction	*n.* the course along which something could move *syn.* way	
perceive	*v.* to know of something through one of the five senses *syn.* sense	
combination	*n.* a thing that is the result of many things put together *syn.* composition	
represent	*v.* to present something or convey a meaning in the form of a sign *syn.* symbolize	
immediately	*adv.* happening right away without any time being lost *syn.* instantly	
individual	*adj.* existing as an unique entity	
turn on	to cause to begin functioning	
give off	to send out or away from	
make up	to constitute	

Unit 4

Word	Definition	Translation
producer	*n.* a living thing (like a plant) that makes its own food and can be used for food	
organism	*n.* a living thing	
consumer	*n.* a living thing that must eat other living things as food in order to live	
decomposer	*n.* a living thing that consumes and breaks apart dead matter	
bacterium	*n.* a very small living thing which often causes a disease *pl.* bacteria	
fungus	*n.* a living thing that consumes decaying matter *pl.* fungi	
tissue	*n.* a group of cells that form parts of living things	
path	*n.* a course along which some process occurs	
sustain	*v.* to allow to continue happening or living	
transfer	*v.* to move or change the positioning of something in relation to something *syn.* shift	
nutrient	*n.* a substance that contributes to the health of a living organism	
visualize	*v.* to make a picture in the mind	
demonstrate	*v.* to prove or make an example by visual means *syn.* show	
maintenance	*n.* the process by which something is kept in good condition *syn.* upkeep	
primary	*adj.* basic *syn.* fundamental	
connected	*adj.* joined together *syn.* linked	
creature	*n.* a living thing *syn.* organism	
constantly	*adv.* not changing or stopping	
depend (rely) on	to require support from some source	
in addition to	over and above	
break down	to decompose or divide into parts	

Unit 5

Word	Definition	Translation
recipe	*n.* instructions for making a certain food	
topping	*n.* something you put on top of food to make it look good or to add flavor	
savory	*adj.* tasty, but not sweet	
buckwheat	*n.* a small grain used for making flour	
batter	*n.* a mixture that usually contains flour and milk or water and is used for cooking	
lentil	*n.* a small bean-like seed that can be eaten	
whisk	*v.* to mix quickly so that air is added	
spatula	*n.* a flat kitchen tool mostly used to turn things over while cooking	
customary	*adj.* often done and practiced since old times *syn.* usual	
ritual	*n.* an event or process that is done in the same way repeatedly *syn.* ceremony	
competition	*n.* an event between two or more rivals to determine which is best at something *syn.* contest	
stir	*v.* to mix in a circular motion	
ingredient	*n.* something that is put into a mixture or recipe	
comparable	*adj.* having features or characteristics similar to someone or something else	
annual	*adj.* occurring once every year	
lack	*v.* to be without *syn.* miss	
assortment	*n.* a group of various things	
nonetheless	*adv.* however; still	
in terms of	describing something as measured by something else	
call for	to list as something needed for a recipe	
be accompanied by	to happen or be present alongside	

Unit 6

Word	Definition	Translation
stilt	*n.* one of two wooden sticks that has a place for the foot and is used to raise a walking person	
knucklebones	*n.* an ancient game played with five small objects which are thrown up and caught	
drape	*v.* to cause cloth to hang or fold over something	
locket	*n.* a piece of jewelry with a small space for holding things, generally worn around the neck on a chain	
charm	*n.* a small object designed to protect its owner, often worn on a necklace or bracelet	
sew	*v.* to join together with needle and thread	
weave	*v.* to use an interlacing pattern to make clothing or baskets	
literature	*n.* artful and expressive writing	
socialize	*v.* to interact with other people	
typical	*adj.* in the manner of the normal *syn.* regular	
observe	*v.* to watch and note changes *syn.* see	
accept	*v.* to allow to become a part of *syn.* approve	
formal	*adj.* following structure and tradition	
responsibility	*n.* something done with the belief that is the proper thing to be done *syn.* duty	
occasion	*n.* an occurrence which does not often happen *syn.* incident	
include	*v.* to contain something as a part of a whole	
provide	*v.* to make things available to someone *syn.* supply	
manage	*v.* to be in charge	
ward off	to keep away	
be supposed to	intended for the purpose of	
according to	referring to information from	

Unit 7

Word	Definition	Translation
identity	*n.* the qualities that make a person or group what they are	
population	*n.* a group of living organisms that share certain traits	
revolution	*n.* a sudden, complete change in government *syn.* rebellion	
hardiness	*n.* the quality of being able to withstand difficulties *syn.* robustness	
solidarity	*n.* agreement between all the members in a group, resulting from their shared beliefs *syn.* unity	
crescent	*n.* the shape of the moon when less than half of it is visible	
Christianity	*n.* a religion based on the teachings of Jesus Christ	
origin	*n.* where something comes from *syn.* beginning	
identical	*adj.* appearing to be exactly the same	
honor	*n.* the quality of always acting in the correct manner *syn.* integrity	
unity	*n.* the quality of being connected through shared beliefs	
respectively	*adv.* in the order listed	
vary	*v.* to change from time to time *syn.* differ	
recognize	*v.* to identify clearly *syn.* realize	
glimpse	*v.* a brief sighting	
intent	*n.* reason for doing something *syn.* purpose	
coincidence	*n.* an instance of two things happening at the same time	
form	*v.* to bring into existence	
stand for	to symbolize	
for instance	for example	
result from	because of	

Unit 8

Word	Definition	Translation
vibration	*n.* repetitive shaking while staying in one place *syn.* quiver	
particle	*n.* a tiny piece of matter	
ripple	*n.* a small wave on the surface of water	
length	*n.* a measured distance or duration	
texture	*n.* the way the surface of something appears to the eyes and to the touch	
ultrasound	*n.* sound that is above the range that humans can hear	
moth	*n.* a kind of insect that is similar to a butterfly but duller in color	
prey	*n.* an animal that may be eaten by another animal	
grab	*v.* to grasp suddenly *syn.* take	
detail	*n.* a specific trait that is part of something larger *syn.* particular	
invisible	*adj.* unable to be seen	
species	*n.* a specific kind of animal *syn.* sort	
navigate	*v.* to make one's way along a journey	
reach	*v.* to travel as far as	
determine	*v.* to conclude what something is after having observed it and thought about it *syn.* decide	
escape	*v.* to avoid or get away from some bad situation *syn.* evade	
effective	*adj.* producing a desired result *syn.* efficient	
tap	*v.* to hit something lightly	
make sense of	to understand	
in other words	expressed another way	
have the ability to	able to do something	

Unit 9

Word	Definition	Translation
infection	*n.* the invasion of the body by germs	
antibacterial	*adj.* fighting or stopping the growth of bacteria	
mucus	*n.* a slippery bodily fluid	
enzyme	*n.* a chemical substance produced by living cells that contributes to important chemical reactions in the body	
digest	*v.* to change food into energy and waste	
antibody	*n.* any of various substances in the body that fights infection	
swelling	*n.* an instance in which a part of the body becomes larger	
lymph gland(node)	*n.* a tissue mass in the body that helps fight infection by catching foreign particles	
germ	*n.* a life form that is too small to be seen that causes illness *syn.* pathogen	
invader	*n.* someone or something that enters by force	
recognition	*n.* the act of knowing or identifying someone or something	
substance	*n.* that which takes up space and has mass; stuff *syn.* matter	
recollection	*n.* the act of remembering	
witness	*v.* to see something happen *syn.* observe	
detect	*v.* to become aware of *syn.* perceive	
function	*v.* to be in action *syn.* operate	
obstruct	*v.* to keep something out *syn.* block	
advance	*adj.* done ahead of time	
fight off	to fight against or keep away	
lock up	to keep something in a place	
carry out	to complete	

Unit 10

Word	Definition	Translation
athletic	*adj.* having to do with sports	
sacred truce	*n.* a highly special and respected agreement to stop fighting for a period of time	
spectator	*n.* a person who watches an event or game	
sprint	*n.* a (usually) short run at the highest speed possible	
chariot	*n.* an ancient wagon with two wheels that was drawn by a horse	
contestant	*n.* a person who competes in a contest	
spear	*n.* a weapon with a sharp end attached to a long stick	
laurel wreath	*n.* a circle of leaves or branches that symbolizes victory, and was worn by the winner of a competition	
accuracy	*n.* the quality of being as near as possible to some ideal or goal	
practice	*v.* to do something regularly or habitually	
allot	*v.* to give some portion of	
reminder	*n.* an act or message meant to help someone remember	
significance	*n.* the importance of something	
territory	*n.* land that is under the control of a government *syn.* dominion	
attempt	*v.* to make an effort to do something *syn.* try	
independent	*adj.* not being controlled by others *syn.* self-governing	
bar	*v.* to not allow to enter or take part in *syn.* exclude	
regard	*v.* to consider someone or something in a particular way	
be based on	founded on, begun in a certain way	
be made up of	consisting of	
be preceded by	having something that has come before	

Unit 11

Word	Definition	Translation
pest	*n.* an insect or animal that is harmful to humans	
plumbing	*n.* a system of drains and pipes that bring in and take away water and gas	
fortify	*v.* to make something stronger in order to protect it	
ditch	*n.* a long, narrow channel that is dug into the ground, usually as a way to direct water or divide land	
armory	*n.* a place where an army's weapons are kept	
treasure house	*n.* a place where valuables are kept and protected	
orchard	*n.* an area where fruit or nut trees have been planted	
tournament	*n.* a competition in which players compete against each other in a series of games until there is one winner	
evolve	*v.* to slowly change	
architecture	*n.* the art of making buildings	
construct	*v.* to build something by combing different parts to form a whole	
besides	*prep.* along with	
eventually	*adv.* in the end	
chamber	*n.* an enclosed area in a building *syn.* room	
surrounding	*adj.* the quality of something being around something on all sides *syn.* encircling	
structure	*n.* something that is built for some purpose *syn.* construction	
artificial	*adj.* not produced by nature *syn.* fake	
feast	*n.* a large, special meal for many people	
give rise to	to lead to the development of	
go about	to approach or deal with something in a certain manner	
be replaced by	to take the place of	

Unit 12

Word	Definition	Translation
term	*n.* a name used to describe a concept	
ownership	*n.* the act of having something as property	
stockholder	*n.* a person who owns shares of a company	
debt	*n.* the state of needing to repay another party	
loan	*n.* money lent with interest charged	
dividend	*n.* a part of a company's profit that is paid to the people with shares in it	
aggressively	*adv.* done in a bold way	
cautious	*adj.* careful to avoid risks	
investor	*n.* someone who lends money in the hope that they will make a profit	
available	*adj.* able to be used or included	
guarantee	*n.* a promise that something will happen	
overall	*adj.* everything considered in total *syn.* general	
perform	*v.* to act according to expectation *syn.* function	
trading	*n.* the activity of buying and selling in business and finance *syn.* commerce	
doubt	*v.* to not be sure that things are as they appear *syn.* distrust	
acquire	*v.* to come to have *syn.* get	
benefit	*n.* to be useful or profitable to *syn.* gain	
expand	*v.* to increase in size, number or importance	
in theory	according to ideas about what could be	
be wary of	be cautious of	
come out ahead	to finish something with benefit to one's self	

Unit 13

Word	Definition	Translation
float	*v.* to stay at the top of a liquid	
sink	*v.* to drop to the bottom of a liquid	
density	*n.* the amount of matter per unit of space	
molecule	*n.* the smallest unit of a substance that is composed of at least two atoms	
experiment	*n.* a test done to learn something or to find out if something works or is true	
jar	*n.* a ceramic or glass container, usually used for storing food	
fresh water	*n.* water that is not salty	
dissolve	*v.* to spread out within a liquid	
opposite	*n.* something that is in direct opposition to some other thing	
compare	*v.* to say how two things are alike	
determine	*v.* to conclude what something is after having observed it and thought about it *syn.* decide	
bottom	*n.* the lowest point	
notice	*v.* to perceive something	
predict	*v.* to say what will happen in the future *syn.* foretell	
observation	*n.* the act of noticing something that happens	
displace	*v.* to move something into a different space *syn.* relocate	
slightly	*adv.* to a small degree *syn.* somewhat	
whether	*conj.* should it be the case	
come up with	to think of an idea	
be equal to	the same in amount or quality	
on the other hand	to consider something in another way	

Unit 14

Word	Definition	Translation
atmosphere	*n.* the mixture of gases that is around a planet	
air pressure	*n.* the force exerted by the weight of air	
oxygen	*n.* a colorless gas that is present in air on Earth and needed for most animals and plants to live	
nitrogen	*n.* a colorless gas that forms most of the Earth's air	
canister	*n.* a container that can be used to hold things	
communication	*n.* the act of exchanging information, thoughts, or feelings	
radio equipment	*n.* a piece of electronic equipment that is used to communicate over a distance	
ground controller	*n.* someone who directs airplanes or spacecraft from a place on the ground	
coordinate	*v.* to arrange for the timing of events to work together well *syn.* synchronize	
fluid	*n.* a substance which flows and is not solid *syn.* liquid	
vacuum	*n.* a space which contains no matter	
insulate	*v.* to protect from change in temperature	
expose	*v.* to leave unprotected	
eliminate	*v.* to get rid of *syn.* discharge	
shield	*v.* to shelter from harm *syn.* protect	
fluctuation	*n.* a change in a price, level etc	
capacity	*n.* the quality of having ability *syn.* capability	
potential	*n.* the ability to develop or succeed	
deal with	to take action regarding some situation	
breathe out	to release the breath	
build up	to accumulate	

Unit 15

Word	Definition	Translation
capital	*n.* money or property, especially used to produce more wealth or start a business	
fund	*v.* to provide money for an event, activity, or organization	
venture	*n.* a new business project that involves financial risk	
niche	*n.* a specialized area of demand for a product or a service	
practical	*adj.* relating to that which is useful and can be put into effect	
technically	*adv.* concerning special skills	
financially	*adv.* having to do with money	
risk	*n.* an action attempted that carries with it the chance of failure	
combine	*v.* to put together	
ignore	*v.* to purposely not take notice of	
directly	*adv.* in the manner of something that happens without hesitation	
complicated	*adj.* not simple or direct, difficult to understand	
strain	*n.* a force that puts pressure on something, sometimes causing damage	
commonplace	*adj.* occurring often *syn.* ordinary	
spot	*v.* to see or notice someone or something	
essential	*adj.* basic and important *syn.* fundamental	
manufacture	*v.* to make things on a large scale *syn.* mass-produce	
unify	*v.* to bring together	
make a decision	to decide what to do or to choose	
pass up	to decline to do something	
be tired of	to begin to dislike some situation	

Unit 16

Word	Definition	Translation
creativity	*n.* the ability to think of or create something new	
geographical	*adj.* having to do with geography	
thinker	*n.* a person who thinks carefully about important subjects or produces new ideas	
philosophy	*n.* a particular set of ideas and principles about life	
humanism	*n.* a belief system that sets people at the center and views that people's needs can be satisfied without religious beliefs	
realism	*n.* artistic representation of things as they really are	
astronomer	*n.* a scientist who observes objects in space and how they move	
scientific method	*n.* the process through which scientists collect data to construct an accurate representation of the world	
continent	*n.* a vast geographic area that occupies a plate on the Earth's crust	
curiosity	*n.* the quality of wanting to know about many things	
emphasize	*v.* to call attention to	
encourage	*v.* to support and help to accomplish	
realistic	*adj.* like reality	
consequently	*adv.* as a result *syn.* therefore	
imitate	*v.* to try to be more like some other thing *syn.* copy	
average	*adj.* not unusual *syn.* ordinary	
thoroughly	*adv.* to a great extent *syn.* completely	
contact	*n.* written or spoken communication with someone	
go through	to experience	
as well	also	
due to	because of	

Unit 17

Word	Definition	Translation
revolve	*v.* to move around something along a circular path	
rotate	*v.* to turn around an axis while remaining in place	
solar time	*n.* time measured according to the sun's movement	
reference point	*n.* a point to which other points or lines are referred, usually in terms of distance and direction	
leap second	*n.* a positive or negative second adjusted to UTC that makes it close to astronomical time	
physical boundary	*n.* a mark that shows where one area ends and another starts	
longitude	*n.* the distance east or west of an imaginary line along the Earth's surface running North to South	
pole	*n.* the northernmost or southernmost point on the Earth	
matter	*v.* to be important or to have an effect	
adoption	*n.* the act of putting something into practice	
confusing	*adj.* unclear and hard to understand	
forward	*adv.* towards the front or in advance	
vertical	*adj.* pointing straight up at an angle of 90 degrees to a flat surface	
establish	*v.* to formally begin something *syn.* found	
maintain	*v.* to work to stay at the same level *syn.* keep up	
evenly	*adv.* in equal amounts *syn.* equally	
contain	*v.* to keep within *syn.* hold	
globe	*n.* the earth or a round sphere that represents the earth	
keep track of	to be constantly aware of changes in activity or location	
in relation to	considering another thing when addressing a subject	
lead to	to bring about	

Unit 18

Word	Definition	Translation
propel	*v.* to cause to move forward	
aviation	*v.* the science of making planes fly	
curved	*adj.* not straight; possessing curves	
resistance	*n.* a force which makes a moving object slow down	
streamlined	*adj.* designed to move efficiently and quickly through the air or water	
scale	*n.* an instrument that measures weight	
stable	*adj.* not likely to move or change *syn.* steady	
opposing force	*n.* a power that counteracts some other power	
exceed	*v.* to go past expectations	
likewise	*adj.* in a similar manner *syn.* similarly	
inspire	*v.* to cause to want to do something	
overcome	*v.* to accomplish in spite of opposing forces *syn.* surmount	
delicate	*adj.* easily harmed or torn *syn.* fragile	
conventional	*adj.* in an ordinary manner *syn.* traditional	
generate	*v.* to make *syn.* produce	
involve	*v.* to make someone or something a part of an act or process *syn.* include	
factor	*n.* one of the reasons for some outcome *syn.* contribution	
particular	*adj.* relating to something special or distinct	
slow down	to make less quick	
pull up	to use force to draw something upward	
cut down	to reduce	

Unit 19

Word	Definition	Translation
evolution	*n.* the process in which animals and plants change and develop gradually over a long period of time	
botanist	*n.* a scientist that studies plants	
geology	*n.* a branch of science concerned with the history of the Earth and its physical features	
finch	*n.* a kind of small songbird that has a cone-shaped bill	
specimen	*n.* a sample of something that is to be studied scientifically	
natural selection	*n.* the process through which genes are passed on or eliminated	
reproduce	*v.* to bear offspring	
dominate	*v.* to strongly influence	
fascination	*n.* having a great amount of interest	
expedition	*n.* a journey made for a certain reason	
trait	*n.* an inherited characteristic or behavior	
encounter	*n.* to have interaction with	
reject	*v.* to refuse	
alter	*v.* to cause to be different *syn.* change	
notion	*n.* a fleeting way of thinking about something *syn.* idea	
profession	*n.* the main activity in which someone makes money *syn.* occupation	
proof	*n.* a thing or action showing that something is true *syn.* evidence	
specific	*adj.* relating to one particular thing	
millions of	some number of millions	
over generations	coming to be after many life cycles	
for further study	in order to do more research	

Unit 20

Word	Definition	Translation
chapel	*n.* a building which is used for Christian worship	
sculpture	*n.* the art of making objects out of a material such as stone, wood, or clay	
platform	*n.* a tall, flat structure on which people can stand or work	
mold	*n.* a soft, green or gray substance that grows on old food or on objects that are in warm, wet air	
the apostles	*n.* the group of early Christians who taught and spread the Christian religion	
panel	*n.* a flat and usually rectangular piece of material that forms part of a door, wall, etc.	
Genesis	*n.* the first book of the Bible, which describes how God created the world	
biblical figure	*n.* an important or famous character in or relating to the Bible	
access	*v.* to reach	
obstacle	*n.* something which makes progress difficult	
innovative	*adj.* new and creative	
occupy	*v.* to use in a space so that it cannot otherwise be used	
precise	*adj.* in a sharply defined manner *syn.* exact	
commission	*v.* to assign or hire to do a task *syn.* employ	
crumble	*v.* to fall into small pieces *syn.* disintegrate	
exhausted	*adj.* to have used up all of one's energy *syn.* spent	
neglect	*v.* to not give proper attention to something that warrants attention *syn.* disregard	
onlooker	*n.* a person who watches a public event but does not participate in it	
be known for	to be recognized or celebrated for someone or something	
upside down	with the top side turned to the bottom	
reach out	to extend out	

LEVEL GUIDE NE_Build & Grow Products

Category	Level	Kindergarten	Low Beginner	Beginner	High Beginner	Low Intermediate	Intermediate	High Intermediate	Secondary A	Secondary B	Secondary C	Word Count
	Lexile®	BR~120L	120L~350L		350L~600L		500L~850L		750L~950L		700L~1100L	
	CEFR Level	Pre~A1	A1		A2			B1		B2		
	AR Reading Level (Average)	0.5	1.3	2.0	2.5	3.3	3.7	4.5	5.2	5.8	6.7	
Phonics	Phonics Code											
	Phonics Show											
	Come On, Phonics											
Readers	Show Time Level 1											400~600
	Show Time Level 2											550~1100
	Show Time Level 3											800~1200
Course-book	Come On, Everyone											
Reading	Read It! 30											30~45
	Read It! 40											35~50
	Read It! 50											50~65
	Read It! 60											50~65
	Read It! 80											65~95
	Read It! 100											70~100
	Read It! 150											100~150
	Read It! 200											160~220
	Read It! 250											220~300
	Reading Sketch Starter											30~45
	Reading Sketch											35~65
	Reading Sketch Up											80~100
	Reading Sponge											45~70
	Read & Retell											50~80
	Reading Sense											80~100
	Reading Clue											100~130
	The Basic Way											150~240
	Read to Reach											140~220
	Reading Source											140~200
	The Best Way											230~340
	Reading Peak											190~270
	Read Up											350~500
	Easy Link Starter											20~35
	Easy Link											35~80
	Insight Link Starter											80~120
	Insight Link											120~250
	Subject Link Starter											90~135
	Subject Link											140~360
	Subject Link Starter 2nd Edition											90~135
	Subject Link 2nd Edition											140~290

Category	Level	Kindergarten	Low Beginner	Beginner	High Beginner	Low Intermediate	Intermediate	High Intermediate	Secondary A	Secondary B	Secondary C	Word Count
	Lexile®	BR~120L	120L~350L		350L~600L		500L~850L		750L~950L		700L~1100L	
	CEFR Level	Pre-A1	A1		A2			B1		B2		
	AR Reading Level (Average)	0.5	1.3	2.0	2.5	3.3	3.7	4.5	5.2	5.8	6.7	
Listening	Listening Stage Starter											
	Listening Stage											
	Listening Stage Plus											
	Listening Seed											
	Listening Season											
	Listening Planner											
Writing	Write It! Beginner											
	Write It!											
	Write It! Paragraph to Essay											
	Write Right Beginner											
	Write Right											
	Write Right Paragraph to Essay											
Speaking	Speaking Stage Starter											
	Speaking Stage											
	Speaking Stage Plus											
	Everyone, Speak! Kids											
	Everyone, Speak! Beginner											
	Everyone, Speak!											
Grammar	중학 영문법 Link											
	요즘 초등 영문법											
	Grammar Stage Starter											
	Grammar Stage											
	Grammar Stage Plus											
	Grammar Ten 기초											
	Grammar Ten 기본											
	Grammar Ten 완성											
	Grammar Space Kids											
	Grammar Space Beginner											
	Grammar Space											
	Grammar in Mind											
	Grammar in Focus											
	Grammar Effect											
Voca-bulary	Word Up											400~1200
	요즘 초등 영단어											216~222
Assess-ment	RADIX Reading / Listening for the TOEFL iBT Blue & Black											